WHEN FAIRY TALE ROMANCES BREAK REAL HEARTS

A Guide to Creating Loving Lasting Relationships

Kimberley Heart

H J KRAMER INC
Tiburon, California

Dedicated to the one who never gave up hope,
who finally found me,
and with whom I am going home.

Published by H J Kramer Inc.
P.O. Box 1082
Tiburon, CA 94920

Cover Design: Spectra Media
Composition: Classic Typography
Book Production: Schuettge & Carleton
Edited by Nancy Grimley Carleton
Manufactured in the United States of America
10 9 8 7 6 5 4 3 2 1

Library in Congress Cataloging-in-Publication Data
Heart, Kimberley.
    When fairy tale romances break real hearts : a guide to creating
loving, lasting relationships / Kimberley Heart.
    p. cm.
Includes bibliographical references.
ISBN 0–915811–39–1 (pbk.) : $12.95
    1. Interpersonal relations. 2. Self-actualization (Psychology)
3. Intimacy (Psychology) 4. Self-actualization (Psychology)—
Problems, exercises, etc. I. Title. II. Title: When fairytale
romances break real hearts.
HM132.H4   1992
158′.2—dc20
                                                            91–58573
                                                                 CIP

Contents

Acknowledgments

To Learn, To Grow, To Change, To Love

When Fairy Tale Romances Break Real Hearts evolved, as I did, over the last seven years. As I grew in depth, so did my manuscript. Although it is true that my growth is a product of my inner drive to know more, this growth would have been fruitless without the love of two very special friends.

This book would never have become a reality without the love of my friends; in fact, much of who I am might not have unfolded without them.

I owe most of what I know about love as well as most of what I know about myself to my friend Lazaris.* Over the last twelve years, he has always been there to love me in the special ways I needed to be loved. Time and time again, as he showed me my own beauty, I learned to believe in myself, always stretching beyond the bounds of who I was, always stretching to be more. Lazaris's light and knowledge are sprinkled throughout this book. So profoundly has he touched my life that all you are about to read and learn can be attributed to

---

*Lazaris is a nonphysical entity, a channeled consciousness without a form. Lazaris is a gentle friend and powerful guide. The Bibliography includes references to the Lazaris Material.

him and to his love for me. Thank you, Lazaris; I will love you always.

The actual creation of this book into a form that is readable and that makes sense is a gift of my friend Katina. For five years now, she has attempted to make a writer out of me. She believed in me and never once gave up. Thank you, Katina. I love you, and thank you for never turning me away, for never letting me down.

Chapter One
Love: The Myth and the Magic

In the beginning, before I learned to distrust myself, to doubt my motives—before the sun set on my first heartbreak—in the very beginning, there was love. Yet somewhere in the untold dramas and mysteries of my life, I allowed it to escape. I remember catching glimpses, like fireflies on a hot summer night, of that bright, burning glow we call love. But all too often when I reached out to grab it, love would disappear somewhere beyond my grasp.

The days would pass into nights and, in the safe confines of my home, I would condemn myself for my inability to hold onto the one thing I wanted most—love. This became a vicious cycle: The greater my self-condemnation, the less worthy I felt of receiving love; the less worthy I felt of receiving love, the greater my self-condemnation. The more I thought about it, the angrier I became.

I am a trained psychotherapist, able to help people with their problems, able to effectively touch their hearts and to help them grow. Why, then, was maintaining a successful relationship as difficult for me as it was for everyone else? I had developed communication skills. I knew—at least I thought I did—what it took to have a successful relationship. So what was wrong with me?

1

The more I thought about it, the more frustrated I became, until I was rarely at peace. During all my years of schooling, seminars, and practical application, I cannot remember anyone ever teaching me the secrets of a loving relationship, so I decided to search for that knowledge on my own.

Myth or Magic?

Discovering the truth about loving relationships was not a direct path for me. It curved around corners, went straight down cliffs, and often folded back upon itself.

I began by exploring our popular beliefs about romantic relationships. These cultural commonalities are more elusive than perhaps we ever realized. They are molded in part by such subtleties as the books we read, the music we listen to, and the T.V. and movies we watch. The deeper I delved into the phenomena of culture, the more I began to understand the myth we had conspired to perpetrate.

Happily Ever After?

In my private practice, I observed intelligent, articulate individuals speak of the latest studies concerning the "New Man" or the "Woman of the 90s." Like starving children, my clients devoured any new information about the opposite sex. My female clients read everything I suggested, from books like *Male Sexuality* by Bernie Zilbergeld to *The Peter Pan Syndrome* by Dr. Dan Kiley.

Just as diligent in their quest to understand women, my male clients read selections such as *The Hite Report* by Shere Hite, *Smart Women, Foolish Choices* by Dr. Cowan and Dr. Kinder, and some even tackled *The Mists of Avalon* by Marion Zimmer Bradley.

All of us were amazed that this newfound "knowledge" did not help. Once we were actually involved in a loving relationship with another human being, we reverted to our preprogrammed cultural behavior. Clearly, we are all caught up in what Dr. Lucinda McDermott terms "Prince-Princessing"—"Interactions between two or more people based on the socially acquired cues usually sent by the opposite sex to which we involuntarily respond chemically, emotionally and behaviorally" (McDermott, 1989). This phenomenon basically encompasses the automatic, preprogrammed behavior we have learned as appropriate to our specific sexual role. This type of behavior is culturally instilled, socially accepted, and therefore incredibly insidious because most of us never even notice how we act or what we say. We play out our male/female roles without questioning what we are doing or why.

To me, this means we have embraced the myth and attempt to live our lives utilizing the princes and princesses that centuries of fairy tales have given us as role models.

Think about it, how many women are "Sleeping Beauties," trying to control the men in their lives with their brains, their beauty, or their naïveté? Or how many "Rapunzels" do you know—women who expect men to take the lead and show them the way out of their lonely towers, women who depend on men to make the world safe? The fact is, most women are probably a conglomeration of Sleeping Beauty and Rapunzel, along with Cinderella, Guinevere, and quite a few others.

Men, on the other hand, are the cultural counterparts, the handsome young princes, the stunning knights in shining armor, or so we have been led to believe. At the same time, many men find themselves playing roles such as the jester. They play the fool, while observing everything, manipulating women into managing their lives for them. Still others might tend more toward Mordred, controlling with hurtful anger and deceptions.

It appears that we have been unwittingly encultured to the myth. We truly expect to live happily ever after in the faded, yellowing pages of mutually accepted lore.

It is easy to understand how this unthinking, unaware

behavior can lead to relationships based on fairy tales rather than on the unique individual each of us is. We are all trained from birth to enhance and perpetuate the myth of romantic relationships rather than to honor our own authenticity and integrity. Why? Simply because we are afraid of what we do not know.

Instead of creating something that would honor our uniqueness (and perhaps be less socially acceptable), we continue to repeat old patterns and therefore create unfulfilling relationships. Until now, we have lacked the courage, willingness, and perhaps the knowledge to risk challenging the myth, because we feared social rejection, we feared failure, and we feared the unknown.

When we embrace the myth, we lose access to the magic. Unknowingly, we weave and reweave the same old web of make-believe and we futilely try to get other human beings to stick to our webs. Unfortunately, the myth only takes us farther from our unique individuality, leaving us confused by the known, frightened of the unknown, and yearning desperately for the *magic*.

Do You Believe in Magic?

Unlike the myth that is perpetrated upon us, what I refer to as *magic* comes from within. This is the reason we yearn for it even though we might not have experienced it yet. The *magic* radiates from our very center because it is who and what we truly are, not the mythical character that we have been taught to believe we are. When we finally discover the *magic*—the power within—it shines like a beacon for others to share.

Yes, I believe in *magic*, and this book is about the *magic* that is uniquely you and me.

And So It Begins

Like many of you, I was seeking a fairy tale relationship. But I was also in search of that unknown *magic* I innately knew existed—that intangible energy that makes life worth living. Since I did not know where to find it, I searched for a man who would be willing to explore the secrets of a magical relationship with me. I searched for a man who would fly across the skies with me on a winged horse.

If this sounds like the stuff of which dreams are made, you are right. You see, I am a dreamer and I believe life can be imbued with light-filled wonder. I believe in our power and greatness as human beings. I believe in our goodness, and I especially believe in our ability to create anything and everything we really want. Therefore, it is not surprising that the driving force behind my search for a magical relationship was just that—the relationship I had always dreamed of.

Sharing my dreams, my search, and the relationship I describe here is not something I do lightly! Doing so opens the pages of my life for scrutiny and judgment. This is frightening. Yet, for me, it is more frightening to allow dreams to fade away into the mists, never to be explored, developed, or dreamed again. So, I will share my dreams with you, hoping to illustrate how this relationship gave me the opportunity to learn, to grow, to search for more understanding of myself—to find the *magic* in that unfathomable dream we call "relationship."

Jonathan

How many times have you had a friend tell you about a new lover? How handsome, brilliant, warm, witty, and charming he is. How beautiful, sophisticated, and intelligent she is. Then comes the day when you are finally introduced to this paragon of manhood or womanhood. You are amazed—the lover is a mess! What can your friend see in him or her, you wonder.

It continues to delight me as I experience this phenomenon over and over again with my women friends, my men friends, my clients, and myself. We all see our lovers as Apollo or Venus because—as we have always heard—our eyes are blinded by love. In reality, however, what truly makes all of our lovers so incredibly special is that they are human—just like you and me.

As we weave our way through *When Fairy Tale Romances Break Real Hearts,* I have chosen to use the name Jonathan to designate the man who shared this adventure with me. For the purposes of confidentiality and the respect I hold for others, I have taken the liberty of changing some of the details about Jonathan and our relationship.

Living the Myth

Like most everyone else, I was adept at creating mythical beginnings. However, also like everyone else, I wanted to make the feelings of love last and even grow—not fade as they had so many times in the past. As we stumble through the jungle maze of my memories together, you will see that this beginning, like many of yours, reads like a modern-day fairy tale.

I remember clearly the first time I saw him. It was in the parking lot of the convention center where I was to attend a daylong seminar. Like many princesses of long ago, I remember thinking that there was something very special about this handsome blond man from the first moment I saw him. He embodied all the qualities that attracted me to a man. He was handsome. His sports car as well as his clothes spoke of money and success. But even more specifically, his casual, almost indifferent attitude toward me when I introduced myself was an alluring challenge.

This, then, was my image of romance. I never questioned *why* I felt as I did; I simply proceeded on raw, unfiltered emotion.

Of course, as fate and the fairies would have it, by the seminar's evening session, I found myself seated next to this man, whose name I soon learned was Jonathan. We spoke during the breaks and began to learn about each other. Soon it became apparent that the attraction I felt was shared, and we were drawn closer and closer together.

We managed to join mutual friends for a late snack after the seminar and spent the entire time enraptured with each other. Since I had no glass slipper, the witching hour came and went, and by the time we checked our watches, it was four A.M. This, I remember thinking, must be love. So, following the custom of our time and space we went home . . . together.

Once again, the circumstances, the setting—everything was like a scene from a screenplay only I could have written. With a full moon sailing high above his beachfront cottage, he created a fantasyland with candlelight, flowers, and a cozy goose-down comforter.

"Once upon a time . . . "? A modern-day fairy tale? Perhaps. Or was it merely the way too many of use choose to fall haphazardly, unwittingly in love?

The next morning, I remember laughing sardonically at myself. I knew that I had fallen in love. I also knew that modern, educated, enlightened women like myself do not fall in love at first sight. Somewhere in the far reaches of my consciousness, I knew there was more to love and relationship. Thus, this budding relationship became my impetus to discover what it was all about.

So my heart took wing and learned to fly with this thing called love. The problem was my heart had not yet learned to navigate those chartless skies. Still, my hunger to know was greater than my fear of getting lost.

I needed to know about love and life, about magic and sex, about men and women—about all the things no one had ever taught me. I needed to know, just as I needed to breathe. So I walked, fell, flew, and danced from one path onto another— always learning, always growing, always moving on.

Like the Phases of the Moon, We Continually Change

I knew that if I wanted my budding relationship with Jonathan to work, I would have to change, to grow. However, at the beginning of my search, I did not even know what growth was. So I went in search of the very essence of myself.

I did not yet realize that my old patterns had only created failure and pain in my life. But I did know that one definition of insanity was to continue to repeat old patterns, while naively expecting different results. So, I promised myself I would discover the parts of me that no longer served me, that no longer honored me, and change them.

I invite you to make the same commitment to yourself. The relationship I explore in this book was my motivating force. Yours might be quite different. Whatever has brought you here, I welcome you, and I applaud your courage. Together, you and I will traverse the pathways of change. It is our willingness to change, to create more in our lives, that creates the true miracles. It is our undying desire to grow, to be more than we currently are, that creates life's *magic!*

The Need to Grow

During my quest to create *magic* in my life through growth and change, I developed skills that have proved indispensable to me. Many of these skills have made my journey of self-discovery much easier. It is my intent to share these skills with you, and to help you create the most powerful growth experience possible. When we grow, parts of us can change. It is my hope that this book will help your changes be deep and long lasting. In order to achieve this goal, I will take time now to explain how this book is organized so you can follow the exercises with ease.

Over the years, I have learned that my private practice

usually reflects my own life, and I find that my clients teach me as much as I teach them. Though I share some of the insights I have learned from my clients in this book, I have altered names, distinguishing characteristics, and specific circumstances in respect for the confidentiality of those involved.

Homegrowth*

Homegrowth exercises follow most major sections of this book. These are carefully arranged exercises that help you discover or rediscover various aspects of yourself. Each exercise builds on the previous one. Each chapter lays a foundation for the ones to follow. The Homegrowths allow you to discover your own personal and unique answers.

From time to time, as you progress through each chapter, you might want to go back and recheck the results you achieved from previous Homegrowths. You might be surprised to find that in a very short time, your answers to some of these exercises will change. As you begin to change, your life will reflect that.

Visualization/Meditation

One of the fastest ways to grow is to get your subconscious mind to help you. You can achieve this by first learning a language your subconscious mind understands, then by creating an interest. (We will discuss the subconscious mind more in Chapter Two.) Currently, I believe the best way to achieve these goals is to use visualization or meditation.

---

*Language is a powerful thing. It is a tool we use to define who we are at any given moment. Dr. Timothy Leary said, "Words are a freezing of reality." Since our purpose here is *change,* it is sometimes necessary to create language that speaks to our changing needs. Like ourselves, words can develop, grow, and change to better describe our evolving thoughts, beliefs, attitudes, and feelings. Although *Homegrowth* is not yet recognized as a word, it conveys what I want to express better than any existing word or words.

Meditation is simply one way to get our minds to slow down in order to absorb information more clearly, thereby allowing us to discover more about ourselves. However, slowing down our minds takes practice.

My Brain Does What?

Perhaps describing the various levels of brain wave frequencies will help demonstrate how functional meditation can be. Most of the time, our brains operate at a frequency referred to as Beta, which is simply the term scientists have assigned to brain wave frequencies that range from fourteen to twenty-four cycles per second (cps). More directly, Beta is the constant "yama-yamaing" that goes on inside our brains. Remember the times your brain would not shut up all night? Well, that was Beta. Perhaps at night, when the world is still, it is easier to recognize how oppressive and destructive this state of consciousness can be when allowed to go unchecked.

Lower brain wave frequencies are referred to as Alpha and Theta. Theta is a brain wave frequency of five to eight cps, while Alpha is generally considered to be from nine to twelve cps. Alpha is the level of frequency we usually use for meditation.

I like to think of Alpha in the following way: Picture your mind as a fertile field just waiting to be cultivated. When there is a lot of bad weather, it is difficult to plant seeds that will take hold and grow. We can call this "bad weather," or distraction, Beta. However, when the weather is calm and the brain is slowed down, as it is during the Alpha state, it is easier to plant seeds that take hold.

In Alpha, we can plant seeds—or suggestions—at a shallow level, where they will come to fruition rapidly. But, because these seeds are planted at a shallow level, repetition or reinforcement is necessary to facilitate growth. Sometimes, for one plant to come to full maturity, we might have to plant four or five seeds. In other words, as we learn the language of our subconscious mind, it is helpful to repeat the meditation. Through repetition, our subconscious understands our request and begins to implement the changes.

Though Alpha is often used for meditation, we also use Alpha at many other times in our lives. For example, much of our T.V. watching is done in Alpha. This is one of the reasons T.V. can be so influential—and perhaps even dangerous. Without conscious awareness, our brains slow down, and thus we are more susceptible to receiving whatever information is being presented to us. Clearly, it is easy to understand how Alpha can intensify the fertility of our brains.

Theta, too, is a very helpful brain wave state and more analogous to planting seeds deep within the ground. It may take longer for evidence of the planted seed to appear, but the roots will be deeper and stronger than those planted in Alpha. Theta is useful in healing the body of pain, hurt, or fear. It is a deep state of consciousness, similar to that of sleepwalking.

Two Types of Meditation

Now that we have a better understanding of the various levels of consciousness, we can discuss the two basic kinds of meditation: *guided meditation* and *clear mind meditation*.

Guided meditation is a team effort between you and the person leading the meditation, whether in person or tape-recorded. Guided meditation can take us on a journey filled with color, sound, smell, touch, taste, and feelings. If the meditation is good, it will utilize as many senses as possible and as many feelings as are appropriate. This is my favorite kind of meditation and undoubtedly the most fun.

I have chosen to use guided meditation in this book because I have found it to be one of the fastest, most powerful avenues to change. The two meditations given in the Meditation Appendix are examples of this.

For the sake of clarity, I will mention briefly the second

type of meditation. *Clear mind meditation* is used to clear the mind of all thought. There are many ways to achieve this, and I have included a list of some of the books that explain this type of meditation in the Bibliography. I believe that clear mind meditation is helpful when used along with guided meditation.

Reaping the Benefits

The secret to the success of any meditation is the depth and intensity of emotion. Feelings are the conduit between us and our subconscious mind. Our emotions tell our subconscious mind that we want to communicate with it. In fact, our feelings are the only way our subconscious mind can differentiate between benign daily existence and our intent to communicate with it.

However, meditation in itself is not a panacea. Meditation alone can only accomplish so much. That is why it is important to use meditation in conjunction with other tools. This is the purpose of the Homegrowths in each chapter. It is essential to complete the Homegrowths *before* moving on to the guided meditations, which are presented in detail in the Meditation Appendix. It is the synergy of these tools—the Homegrowths and the meditations—that creates lasting change.

When Fairy Tale Romances Break Real Hearts is not only about romantic relationships, but perhaps more importantly, it is about our relationship with ourselves. In the following chapters, you and I will explore uncharted pathways into ourselves. As we would in a journey through the tropical jungles of the Amazon, we will discover exquisite wonders as well as scary monstrosities we would just as soon ignore. Together, we will look at the parts of ourselves we would rather turn away from and celebrate the parts that reflect our wonder. Welcome to the journey!

Chapter Two
Life Lessons

New concepts are not always easy for me. Perhaps they are not easy for anyone. However, I knew I would never have the relationship I wanted with Jonathan unless I was willing to accept the possibility that my old concepts and ideas about relationships might be erroneous. It was clear to me that, without conscious effort, I had become an expert on what did not work. This time, however, I was determined not to repeat the same old patterns.

Still, knowing what did *not* work left me no closer to what did. So, I continued to stumble over, bump into, and fall upon many of my old behaviors, until I finally realized that simply *noticing* what did not work was an important lesson in itself.

That's right—simply noticing how old patterns of behavior no longer served me opened up new ways of seeing my old problems and behaviors. As time passed, I found that recognizing old ways of being actually opened the doorway to discovering new ideas. These new ideas seemed to have an uncanny way of leading me toward more life-enhancing challenges.

A new adventure was beginning for me, an adventure that would ultimately lead to creating *magic*.

Our Beliefs Create Our Experiences

Maybe wishing won't make it so, but *believing* will. I still remember the misty Friday night in Mill Valley, California, when I first heard an innovative concept about beliefs and belief systems. I was attending a weekend seminar given by my new friend Lazaris,* sponsored by Concept: Synergy, an organization dedicated to the development of the human spirit.

"Your beliefs create your experiences." The impact of those words was immediate. I felt a dull thud in my abdomen as the words reached my conscious mind. The implications of that statement were staggering. When the statement was made again—"Your beliefs create your experiences"—it hit me with full force. In fact, I was so intrigued with this statement that those exact words continued to reverberate in my mind during the entire presentation.

Later, as I watched tendrils of fog invade the San Francisco Bay from my hotel window, I thought about those words again. I wondered if my perception of life might be much like this fog. How quickly the fog had engulfed the bay, hiding even the brightest city lights. Had the beliefs I embraced so dearly all my life acted in the same way, blinding me to a new reality?

My mind continued to race. If my beliefs truly did create my experiences, I would have to rethink my entire life. Like most of us, I had always been taught the complete opposite— that my experiences create my beliefs. Now, I was presented with a new way of thinking.

I began to wonder if my beliefs could, indeed, create my experiences. I fumbled through a maze of examples trying

---

*Lazaris is a nonphysical entity, a channeled consciousness without a form. Lazaris is a gentle friend and a wise and powerful guide. The Bibliography contains references to the Lazaris Material.

to make sense of one theory or the other. The pieces churned round and round. Sometimes they seemed to fit; other times they did not. Slowly, I began to realize that perhaps the pieces did not need to fit.

If I *believed* that my experiences created my beliefs, they did. If I *believed* that my beliefs created my experiences, they did. The key words in these two statements are "If I believed." Whatever I believed, *was*. Whatever I believe now, *is*. This new awareness was both powerful and frightening. And with it came total freedom embraced in overwhelming responsibility.

If I, indeed, created my world based on my beliefs, then any experience I have ever had was created by me. That meant I, alone, was responsible for what I had created. It also meant I had the freedom to create whatever I chose to believe. Perhaps this is what Anaïs Nin felt when she wrote:

> *So the day I was told by Otto Rank (her psychotherapist in the 1930s) that I was responsible for the failures, the defeats that had happened to me, and that it was in my power to conquer them, that day was a very exhilarating day. Because if you're told that you're responsible that means that you can do something about it. Whereas the people who say society is responsible, or some of the feminist women who say man is responsible, there is nothing you can do. I preferred to take the blame, because that also means that one can act, and it's such a relief from passivity, from being the victim.*

Believing Can Make It So

Once when I was thirteen, my Uncle Howie handed me a cloth bag. He made me guess what was in it before he allowed me to open it. After I guessed several times, he finally allowed me to pour the contents onto the kitchen table. Out tumbled dozens of small, multicolored pieces of cardboard—

a jigsaw puzzle. I looked at him with confusion. There was no picture, just lots of pieces. How was I to know how to put the puzzle together without a picture to guide me?

"I thought it would be lots more exciting to try it without a picture," Uncle Howie said. "Come on, Kimberley, let's try it!"

Trying to understand how my belief systems operated was similar to putting that pictureless puzzle together—frustrating, yet exciting. When I tried to put the pieces of my real-life puzzle together, I began to realize how important beliefs are in forming our reality.

I began to notice examples of this everywhere, but my client Shelly's story is perhaps the most profound example of how our beliefs actually do create our experiences, because her very life depended on her ability not only to recognize but also to understand her beliefs.

When I first saw Shelly, her physician had diagnosed a malignant tumor in her brain. The prognosis was terminal, she had been given only one month to live. She sat across from me, staring out the window to her left.

"The stupid doctor told me that I'm going to die," she said, her eyes studying the fall scene outside. "But I'm not."

Maybe her statement would have sounded ludicrous to her doctor, but it actually saved her life. Shelly simply refused to accept her doctor's beliefs about her life. She began educating herself on every available cure for cancer—from conventional to radical. Intuitively, she chose nonconventional methods of treatment in which she was an active participant—not a victim. However, the most courageous choice Shelly made was her willingness to *believe* that she could and would live. The method by which she honored this belief was incidental; the power came from her belief.

Eagerly, I watched as Shelly began to create a new life for herself, a life her physician thought was over. Shelly's willingness to respond to her belief about her illness saved her life. Perhaps her refusal to put her life into the hands of another was the first step in responding to her own needs. In doing so, she took over the responsibility for creating her life.

"I can't be responsible if you won't do what I say," her doctor would tell her.

"Good," Shelly thought, smiling to herself. "Then I can do exactly what I want to do!" Shelly's new sense of self-responsibility gave her a level of freedom few of us have achieved. The more willing she was to accept responsibility, the more freedom she had. Taking the responsibility to question her doctor's traditional wisdom allowed Shelly the freedom to seek her own wisdom and the power to act in her own best interests.

Would you or I have been willing to take responsibility for our own lives? Would it have been simpler for Shelly to turn her life over to society, her doctor, or to God? Perhaps. However, like Anaïs Nin, Shelly learned that if she accepted the responsibility for what she had created through her beliefs, she then had the power and the freedom to change her beliefs and thus her life.

Now, more than ten years later, Shelly is alive, and for perhaps the first time, she is living life on her own terms.

Slowly, I began to make the connection. Shelly's beliefs were indeed creators. Clearly, our beliefs do create our realities. And through our beliefs, we ourselves become the creators of our own lives.

As the pieces began to fit together, I caught glimpses of the bigger picture. Not only are our beliefs an immense power in our lives, we must be willing to respond to that power in order to gain personal freedom.

Getting What You Want

Isn't that what it's all about—getting what you want? Isn't that why you're reading this book—to get what you want, a successful relationship? Just from the heading of this section alone, you might think, "Oh, the good part. Now she is going to tell us *how to do it*—how to get what we want."

Well, I would like to suggest that we already have what we want. That's right—we already have exactly what we want in our lives at this very moment.

Of course, this only makes sense if we remember our initial premise—*our beliefs create our experiences.* "We have what we want" means that we have what we *believe* is possible and what we *believe* we deserve.

Because we have never been taught to distinguish the difference between what we think and what we believe, most of us are outraged by the statement "We have in our lives what we really want." Because we *think* we want all sorts of things we do not have, learning that we already have what we want may not only sound untrue, it may sound incredibly unfair.

Thinking Is Not Believing

As I mentioned previously, beliefs are an immense power in our lives because they are one of the basic creators of our experiences. However, there are also other creators of our realities, such as our attitudes, thoughts, feelings, choices, and decisions.

For example, we have been told repeatedly to think positively. Why? Because what and how we think actually does affect what happens around us and how other people respond to us.

Yet, if thinking creates our reality, why don't all our thoughts manifest themselves? Because the reality our thinking creates ultimately honors our belief systems. The same is true of our attitudes, feelings, choices, and decisions. They can only create a reality outlined by our beliefs. Beliefs are the major power in our lives.

This is the reason some of our thoughts, such as "This is the beginning of a happy relationship," might not become a reality if our *belief* is "Love hurts," or "I don't deserve to be happy." Our thoughts will ultimately be overridden by our beliefs.

Although our beliefs are among the most powerful, creative

raw materials we have, let's review some of the other elements that work independently and together to create our reality by honoring our beliefs. These elements are attitudes, thoughts, feelings, choices, and decisions. By placing these elements in a diagram, perhaps it will be easier to understand the relationship each of these has to the other.

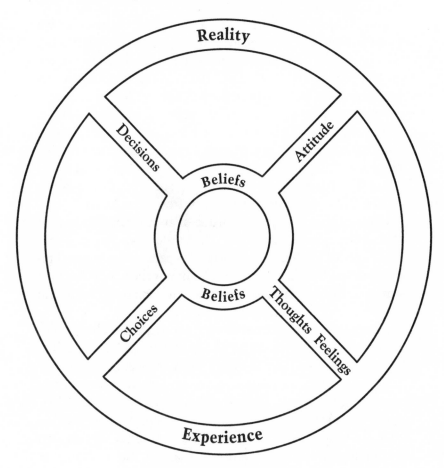

Figure 1: The Wheel of Reality

Since this is a complex concept to grasp, let's picture it like this: Think of a wheel. The hub of the wheel represents our beliefs. The spokes work independently and together to support the outer rim, which represents our experiences or our reality. Let's take a closer look at each spoke in our wheel of reality in order to see how each works to create experiences that honors the hub—our beliefs.

Our *attitudes* are perhaps best described as the color we paint our world. Our attitudes color or prejudice everything we experience. Two people can have identical beliefs (for example, "Love hurts"), yet their individual attitudes can create totally different experiences in the world.

For example, the *attitude* of one person who *believes* "Love hurts" might be "This is just how life is and therefore I must learn to survive and do the best I can." Consequently, this person will create experiences that make the best of a bad thing. Though the belief is love hurts, the attitude allows the creation of a more positive reality from that belief.

On the other hand, the attitude of another person having the identical belief might be, "The world has a personal vendetta against me." Consequently, this person may create embittered and hateful experiences to honor the belief that love hurts. Clearly, individual attitudes can create different life experiences based upon the same belief.

As we have already mentioned, *thoughts* are also powerful creators, as are *feelings*. Each thought and each feeling we have creates a flow of energy that can be consciously utilized to enhance or inhibit our lives. Learning how to use this energy is a skill that would serve us well to develop.

For instance, if we are angry, that is simply a normal human emotion or feeling. What we do with the energy created by our anger creates our reality. We can use the anger to hurt and punish ourselves or others, or allow it to catapult us forward into greater understanding.

We can also learn to harness the energy of our thoughts.

We can use the energy created by a thought ("I can do anything I want with my life") to influence the reality we create for ourselves either positively or negatively.

Our *choices* are strongly influenced by our attitudes, thoughts, and feelings. The multiplicity of choices we allow ourselves is also based on these factors. However, the final *decisions* we make are influenced by all the above factors, including our choices. For instance, if we only allow ourselves the choice between no relationship and a hurtful relationship, we might well make the final decision of having no relationship. Every choice and decision we make creates our reality.

This explains why therapy does not always create permanent change. Changing attitudes, thoughts, feelings, choices, and/or decisions results in a job half done. Now we understand it is our beliefs that must be changed in order to make our lives work better.

The Subconscious Mind

Now that we have learned how our beliefs along with our attitudes, thoughts, feelings, choices, and decisions create our reality, let's take a look at how that marvelous (albeit much maligned) level of consciousness, our subconscious mind, functions in the same process.

Our subconscious mind is functional in creating our reality because it is the storehouse of our beliefs. In order to understand how this works, let's try visualizing our subconscious mind as a huge mainframe computer.

Like all computers, our subconscious mind does exactly what we ask it to do. We have programmed our subconscious mind to store information, including all our beliefs, and to create a reality that honors those beliefs.

It is important to understand, first of all, that our subconscious mind stores *all* the information we encounter. This means absolutely every bit of information—from every street sign we might have read to every dream we ever had, even the ones we think we don't remember. Our subconscious mind stores all this information, saving us the task of having to be consciously aware of everything we know. To better comprehend the enormity of this, imagine memorizing every book in the Library of Congress and keeping all that information current. This is the type of work our subconscious mind does, thus leaving us energy for other, more important, tasks.

The second mammoth job of our subconscious mind is to create experiences in our lives that honor the beliefs we have stored there. Please understand that it is the job of the subconscious to *honor* our beliefs, not to judge or evaluate them.

As we live from moment to moment, our subconscious mind sets our beliefs in motion and the hubs in our wheels— our beliefs—begin to turn. An energy, not unlike a centripetal force, pulls into our reality anything that honors that particular belief.

For instance, let's go back to an earlier example: "Love hurts." The hub of the wheel is the belief "Love hurts." As the wheel spins, its centripetal force pulls in and holds corresponding attitudes, thoughts, feelings, choices, and beliefs:

Attitudes: The opposite sex cannot be trusted.
Thoughts: Every relationship I have ever had ended badly.
Feelings: I feel hurt.
Choices: I choose to have no relationship or one that is hurtful.
Decisions: Romantic relationships are not for me.

If any element that does not honor the belief tries to attach to the hub, that element will be crushed by the forces of the other elements that are attracted by the belief. For example, if a thought such as "I like men" tries to attach itself to the hub and consequently become part of reality, the other elements will override the thought, never allowing it to take hold. Because the thought was never allowed to secure itself to the hub of the wheel, its influence will never manifest itself in reality.

Our subconscious mind stores our beliefs and creates enough energy to see that they are ultimately honored in our reality. It also accesses and utilizes our attitudes, thoughts, feelings, choices, and decisions to continually create a reality that honors the beliefs it stores.

The Subconscious in Action

How do we know what we actually believe? How do we tap into or gain access to our subconscious mind to find the beliefs we have stored there? Let's look at my client Brent's situation to find one avenue toward becoming better acquainted with our own beliefs.

Brent was a young man who shared an apartment with his dog, George, and his roommate, Scott. It was an arrangement that worked for the three of them, until Mary came into Brent's life. Scott didn't have to be a soothsayer to know that Brent and Mary had fallen in love. Brent *thought* Mary was the perfect woman for him. Before long, Mary began spending more and more time at Brent's. In fact, it soon became her routine to have dinner waiting when Brent got home from work.

On one particularly sultry evening, after arguing with his boss and fighting rush-hour traffic, Brent arrived home tired and more than a little crabby. The one bright spot in his day was knowing Mary would be waiting for him. Well, she certainly was, but dinner wasn't what she was keeping warm.

The first time I saw Brent, he had deep circles under his eyes. He had not stopped obsessing since Mary and his *ex*-roommate, Scott, had moved into their own apartment.

This story is not uncommon. Every one of us has experienced heartaches that seemed to appear out of nowhere.

When I suggested to Brent that he was responsible for creating this experience, he looked at me as if I had sprouted green hair.

"Perhaps you really didn't want a relationship with Mary," I probed.

"Are you nuts? She was perfect!" He was incredulous. "Our relationship was perfect . . . now I've got nothing. They're together, and just like always I end up alone." Brent masked his pain with rage.

With help, he realized that the pain he was suffering was familiar, one he had experienced too many times before. So, together we began to explore Brent's painful old patterns.

As Brent and I discussed his relationship with Mary, he kept asking himself the same old questions: "What went wrong?" "Why didn't I know something was wrong?" "How could they do this to me?" "How could Scott?"

His questions only led him in circles, but it didn't take him long to notice that he was getting nowhere.

So, instead of searching for better answers to his old questions, we went in search of new ones—new questions which would lead Brent to discover what his *beliefs* about relationships actually were. Brent needed to find new questions that would help him delve into the intriguing world of his subconscious. It was a path I had already explored in my own attempt to understand my relationship with Jonathan.

Homegrowth 1: Looking for the Questions

(1) Make a list of questions that will help you gain insight into your true desires regarding a romantic relationship.

EXAMPLE:
- What do I lose by having a romantic relationship?
- If I am in a romantic relationship, will I risk being the real me?
- Do I want just one relationship?
- Do I want commitment?

(2) Answer each question in depth.

→ Take the time to really think about the question.

→ Think about the answer just as thoroughly.

To help you get the idea about working with the Home-growth exercises, I will review my answers to the questions used in the example.

What Do I Lose by Having a Romantic Relationship?

Me! Myself! My personhood! I actually believed I would love a man so deeply that I would want to give up everything I was just to be with him. I had seen many women, including my own mother, do this. I had read countless books in which it was imperative for the heroine to give up her own life for the sake of her true love. I had learned the lessons of our culture well: A woman in love should be willing to sacrifice everything for love. I must confess at least a tiny part of me thought this was terribly romantic.

I was in the midst of an internal war. One part of me knew I could never be happy if I gave up my personal wants and desires. The other part believed my only hope for a romantic relationship was to do just that.

The old emotional scripting was strong. It was clear that if I wanted a romantic relationship, I would have to seek a way of having it without losing *anything* at all. I would have to change my enculturated belief that romantic love meant self-sacrifice.

Will I Risk Being the Real Me?

If I believe sharing who I am authentically in a romantic relationship is a risk, then perhaps I am unsure about who I am. Or perhaps, I have judged myself as inadequate or "not enough."

If, indeed, I am unsure about my own identity, it is most likely because I do not want to know more about myself. If I have judged myself as inadequate, it might be because I do not want to discover the truth about myself.

Relationships have a funny way of reflecting us not only to others but back to ourselves as well. Healthy relationships also have a funny way of demanding that we recognize who it is we see in the reflection, that is, who we really are.

If I—for whatever reason—do not want to become better acquainted with myself, then it follows that I truly do not want a romantic relationship.

Do I Want Just One Relationship?

There are several ways of looking at this question. When I began to answer this question, I learned once again just how powerful my beliefs are. I know I only want one relationship at a time. Yet I also know how much I enjoy the excitement of creating new beginnings. I found it interesting to notice that I wanted two things that seemed to be mutually exclusive: a one-man life-style and lots of new beginnings.

This was interesting to me because I began to realize that I had created lots of painful separations from Jonathan simply so I could re-create exciting new beginnings. Without conscious effort, I had fulfilled both my desires and created a reality that honored my beliefs. This was only one more example of why it is critical that we come to know our beliefs because they actually do create our reality.

Another facet of this question that intrigued me was the time element. Did I honestly want only one relationship for the rest of my life? The concept of spending the next eighty years with one individual continued to be overwhelming to me.

Do I Want Commitment?

Damn right I wanted commitment. For me, commitment included monogamy and my partner's positive intent about desiring an exclusive relationship with me. I wanted a commitment of monogamy because I thought it would insure my partner's investment in me and the relationship. The problem with this type of synthetic security is that it does not work. For example, either party, at any time, can change her or his mind. Finally, I began to notice that my need for the big "C" was an illusion. In Chapter Four, we will discover that true, authentic security is actually self-care.

As I explored these and other questions and answers, self-discovery became more and more exciting. The answers opened up even more questions, which, in turn, enabled me to look even deeper within myself, and I continued to increase my list with questions such as:

- Am I willing to take responsibility for my beliefs concerning romantic relationships?
- Am I willing to change the beliefs that no longer serve me?
- Am I willing to embrace new beliefs and create a different reality?

As I added new questions to my Homegrowth assignment, I began to consider my willingness to create a different reality for myself. What exactly would that mean, I wondered? What would my new life be like? Was I willing to have these changes in my life? How would these changes affect everything else in my life?

As you can see, I had begun to master the art of asking questions. I would have to decide—as you will—if I was willing to continue my journey inward.

Exploring new, more honest questions helped me focus on myself and my belief systems. Instead of asking a question that denoted blame or judgment (such as "How could he do this to me?"), I asked questions that helped me probe the inner workings of my subconscious, questions that led me closer to my beliefs.

I was pleasantly surprised to learn that my beliefs were actually quite accessible. Since my beliefs create my reality, I only had to notice what I had (or did not have) in my life to determine what I actually believed. Ever since I learned this lesson, my life has become an open book, constantly displaying my beliefs to me.

Homegrowth 2: Discovering Beliefs

(1) (a) On the far left-hand side of a sheet of paper, make a list of all of the things you currently have in your life that you really want.

 (b) In a second column to the right, list what you must believe in order to have created that reality.

→ Note: The following examples are to help you understand the exercise. You will want to give longer, more detailed answers.

EXAMPLE:

Have and Want	*Belief*
A well paying and enjoyable job	Money is fun to create.

---

(2) (a) On the far left-hand side of a second piece of paper, list all of the things you have but *do not* want.

 (b) In a second column to the right, list what you must believe in order to have created that reality.

EXAMPLE:

Have and Do Not Want	*Belief*
A hurtful romantic relationship	Love hurts.

---

(3) (a) On a third piece of paper, in a column on the far left-hand side, list all of the things you think you want in your life but do not have.

(b) In the next column, in the middle of the page, list all of the reasons you want these things.

(c) In the third column, to the far right, list all of the reasons you do *not* want these things.

EXAMPLE:

What I Want	Why I Want It	Why I Don't Want It
A romantic relationship	To feel close and connected	Fear of vulnerability
To share love and intimacy	It's fun.	Lack of trust

This Homegrowth will help you learn more about what you have created and why you created it. The more thought and feeling you put into this exercise, the stronger start you will have toward understanding your beliefs and the reality you have already created.

Opening the Door to Self-Honesty

By the time Brent reached the third list of his Homegrowth—what he wanted but did not have—he was stumped. Of course, the one thing he wanted—but no longer had—was his relationship with Mary. In the second column, he had listed the usual reasons for wanting this relationship:

Someone to love me
Someone to do things with
Someone to keep me from being alone
Someone to make me feel safe

But his "Why I Don't Want It" column was blank. Consequently, he appeared at my office frustrated and angry with me for giving him the assignment in the first place.

"This is really stupid," he said. "I don't have any reasons for not wanting a relationship with Mary."

By doing this assignment, Brent was testing the theory that we have in our lives what we really want. Now he was finding it difficult to be totally honest with himself. It was difficult to face his true beliefs, and this made him angry.

As he realized he was hiding from himself, thereby creating an internal struggle, he became aware that his anger was directed toward himself. After coming to terms with his anger, Brent learned that his rage was a mask for his fear. He was actually frightened of what he might find stored away in his subconscious mind. This fear led to his inability to be honest about his beliefs until he was hiding them from the one person he needed to be completely honest with—himself!

Brent's process was familiar; I, too, had experienced similar frustration and anger. In my mind, Jonathan was perfect. At first, I couldn't imagine one reason I would not want a relationship with him. Like Brent, I learned if I could not answer the question about why I didn't want the relationship, I was hiding. My anger was a way to hide from myself, to hide from the fear I really felt.

Since I consider myself an adventurer, I charged ahead into that fear. But looking back now, it is easy to see that I had managed to dupe myself. For even when I finally filled in the "Why I Don't Want It" column, my answers were relatively superficial.

Afraid of giving up my independence
Afraid of becoming subservient to a man

My answers did not really address the heart of the matter—my beliefs. By not being willing to look honestly at my beliefs,

I continued to feel frustrated and angry for no apparent reason. By holding on to these feelings, I never had to delve any deeper into my beliefs and take responsibility for the reality I continued to create.

Instead, I continued my relationship with Jonathan, living cleverly with my self-duping. I had convinced myself that I was automatically on the road to a successful relationship simply because I had completed Homegrowth 2, Discovering Beliefs. I foolishly decided that completing the assignment would guarantee a new reality.

I never considered the possibility that I would have to risk being impeccably honest with myself if I wanted to explore and understand my beliefs. Before long, however, the reality I created let me know I would have to take that risk.

Jonathan began complaining about my constant need to be reassured of his love. I was shocked. I considered myself stable and secure and had not realized I needed reassurance. Still, his repeated words began to penetrate until I realized that sometimes, even when he was holding me, I was frightened, and I didn't know why. After all, I had examined my beliefs, and I was creating a new reality—or so I thought.

It took a while before I realized I was continuing to create what I wanted based on my hidden beliefs. It was then I considered taking another look at my Homegrowth exercise. I reexamined my lists, and decided to try the entire exercise one more time—this time with impeccable honesty.

When I reworked the exercise, I was shocked. I discovered that, deep within my subconscious, I had stored many beliefs about love and relationships that kept me from creating the reality I wanted. These were the hidden beliefs that triggered my anger, which masked my fear.

Love Hurts

Discovering I believed being loved would ultimately cause incredible pain was a process, not an instant realization. By being impeccably honest with myself, I was able to take a small step toward this ultimate awareness.

My reasoning went something like this: If I loved Jonathan, I would be vulnerable to any amount of pain. If I was, indeed, vulnerable, then Jonathan would have the power to hurt me. And from what I could tell, it seemed as if I was hurting most of the time. It didn't take me long to make the connection between the pain I created in this relationship and one of my beliefs about love.

When I realized that my unexplained fear was of being hurt, I was appalled but not surprised. My childhood had been such that fear and pain were not uncommon occurrences.

Watching my mother and father "love" each other had fed this belief about love, which I simply stored in my subconscious mind. As I grew, it seemed everyone around me demonstrated love by yelling, screaming, and fighting.

Remembering my past made it easier for me to understand this belief, which I had formed so long ago and stored safely away. Not surprisingly, the reality I created was based on this old belief. If this was love, I decided, who needed it?

I was pleased and gratified at finding this old belief. However, I was gravely mistaken in my fantasy that my fear of being hurt would simply self-destruct once I understood the belief behind it. Jonathan's complaints about my insecurity persisted even after I had identified the belief.

Because I continued to believe that love would hurt, it did. I continued to create my reality based upon my beliefs. I was fascinated by the knowledge that I did not have in my life what I *said* I wanted; I had what I *really* wanted—what I *believed*.

The most empowering part of this realization was that simply identifying the belief was not enough. Realization alone was not enough. If a belief no longer served me, I would have to find a way to change it.

Changing Beliefs

With all this in mind, it clearly stands to reason that if we do not have the successful relationship we say we want, we can learn which beliefs created this, and change those beliefs. One of the most profound lessons of our times is to learn about ourselves and how we can consciously change anything we choose. As we have learned, ultimately all our behaviors, thoughts, and feelings can be traced back to our beliefs. Consequently, this entire book is dedicated to teaching just that— how to change our beliefs.

Although long-lasting change comes from changing our beliefs, we can change our behaviors, thoughts, and feelings as well. Therefore, throughout the book, I have included examples of change in these various arenas.

UnlimitedGrowth* Can
Create Permanent Change

Growth and change are different processes and should not be confused. Only change can create long-lasting differences in us. We can continue to grow by developing insight and accumulating knowledge. However, this new insight and knowledge does not guarantee a difference in our behavior or in how we feel. Growth prepares us to change.

---

*Language is a powerful thing. It is a tool we use to define who we are at any given moment. Dr. Timothy Leary said, "Words are a freezing of reality." Since our purpose here is *change*, it is sometimes necessary to create language that speaks to our changing needs. Like ourselves, words can develop, grow, and change to better describe our evolving thoughts, beliefs, attitudes, and feelings. Although *UnlimitedGrowth* is not yet recognized as a word, it conveys what I want to express better than any existing word or words.

I call the four-step growth process that leads to permanent change UnlimitedGrowth.* UnlimitedGrowth encompasses the entire meaning of this book.

For the sake of clarity, I have outlined the UnlimitedGrowth process in this chapter. Please keep in mind, this is only an outline. As you progress through the book, each chapter presents new skills and tools that are interrelated to and dependent upon those presented in preceding chapters. You will not be able to complete the UnlimitedGrowth process until you acquire these skills and learn to use the tools.

The Homegrowths throughout this book and outlined here are designed to lead you gently into UnlimitedGrowth and Change. They will provide your touchstones on this journey filled with wonder, magic, discovery, and joy. This is your personal adventure into yourself.

UnlimitedGrowth

UnlimitedGrowth is a four-step process that will lead to lifelong change. The first three steps—Notice, Acknowledge, and Forgive—are comprised of one or more Homegrowth exercises expressly formulated to prepare you for the fourth step, lasting Change!

Step One: Notice

In Step One, you will learn how to identify in detail precisely what you want to change. The two Homegrowths you have previously completed have helped you develop a new way of thinking and questioning. These skills will make "noticing" more elegant.

By producing concise and specific statements of your beliefs, the following Homegrowth will give you some insight

---

*Based on The Change Process taught by Lazaris. See Lazaris, *Unlocking the Power of Changing Your Life,* © 1986 NPN Publishing, Inc.

into your beliefs and how you feel about them. These statements will provide the foundation for elegant change as you proceed through UnlimitedGrowth toward change.

Homegrowth 3: You Are What You Believe

In this exercise, we are dealing with your subconscious mind — not your thoughts. The key to the success of this exercise is spontaneity. This means answering each blank in two-thirds of a second. Yes, two-thirds of a second! Once you get the knack, you will be able to recognize when you move out of spontaneity and begin to "think."

It is also important to complete the exercise in the two-part process described, as this fosters a deeper level of communication with your subconscious.

As with all Homegrowths, these responses are for you alone; no one else need ever see them. So be gentle with yourself; try not to judge or censor your responses. Allow the flow of spontaneous communication to create impeccable honesty with yourself.

(1) On five separate sheets of paper, write one of the following headings:

Romantic relationships are . . .
Money is . . .
Sex is . . .
Love is . . .
I am . . .

→ Follow the same instructions for each topic.

(2) Write the numbers 1 through 33 down the left-hand side of each page.

(3) Write as many *one-word* responses as come to your mind — *spontaneously.*

→ Remember: No thinking!

(4) If you do not come up with a response in less than a second, stop. Clear your mind and say the page heading out loud. (For example, "Romantic relationships are . . . ")

→ Write down the first thing that comes into your head.

EXAMPLE:
Romantic relationships are . . .
1. fun
2. hard
3. impossible

---

(5) Complete the list of thirty-three responses for each topic.

→ Do not be concerned if an occasional response is duplicated.
→ If you cannot accomplish this at one sitting, simply come back to it at another time.

(6) After you have completed thirty-three one-word responses for *each* of the five categories, return to the first sheet of paper.
(7) Complete each sentence by adding, "and I feel _____ ."

→ Use the same spontaneous response method described above.

EXAMPLE:
Romantic relationships are . . .
1. *fun* and I feel *happy.*
2. *hard* and I feel *angry.*
3. *impossible* and I feel *helpless.*

---

(8) Repeat this process with each category.

You have just acquainted yourself with some of your beliefs. If you wrote, "Romantic relationships are hard," you carry the belief somewhere in your subconscious that these relationships are difficult for you.

You have also learned how you *feel* about your beliefs. This is vital information you have given yourself because you have begun to *notice*.

Before proceeding to the next Homegrowth, take a closer look at your lists and decide which beliefs no longer serve you, which beliefs you want to change.

Since the category, "I am . . . " has given you an understanding of what you believe and feel about yourself, you might want to focus on it. Before you can successfully change your beliefs in other categories, it is important to understand and embrace what you basically believe about yourself.

Homegrowth 4: Choose and Grow

In this Homegrowth you will delineate exactly which belief you want to change and what you want to change it to.

(1) Choose one belief you want to change and write it on a separate sheet of paper.

(2) Below the belief you want to change, write the new belief you would like to change it to.

→ Use the same grammatical form as the original belief.

→ Note: it is not necessary to change the wording of the new belief to the exact opposite of the belief you want to change.

EXAMPLE:

Old belief: Romantic relationships are hard.
New belief: Romantic relationships are easy.

Old belief: Romantic relationships are impossible.
New belief: Romantic relationships are safe.

These two Homegrowths have helped you complete the first step in UnlimitedGrowth. In this step, you have *noticed* what some of your beliefs are and learned how to evaluate which beliefs you want to change.

Step Two: Acknowledge

You will find the skills and Homegrowth exercises necessary to complete Step Two—Acknowledge—of Unlimited-Growth in Chapter Three. Acknowledging that we have created and maintained beliefs that no longer honor us is a two-phase process. In the first phase, you gain an *understanding* of why you created and maintained your belief by answering in detailed written form the Payoff Questions presented in Homegrowth 8, Exploring the Why, in Chapter 3. In the second phase, you take responsibility for your *impact* by writing about how your belief has had negative impact upon your life and the lives of those you love. Do Homegrowth 9, Impact and Responsibility, in Chapter 3.

Step Three: Forgive

The skills, Homegrowths, and meditation necessary to complete Step Three of UnlimitedGrowth are described in Chapter Three, Homegrowths 8-11. These exercises will guide you in completing Step Three: Forgive.

Homegrowth 5: Finally Free

Complete Meditation 1, Finally Free, located in the Meditation Appendix.

Step Four: Change!

In chapters Four through Seven, you will begin to develop a deeper knowledge of yourself. This part of the journey prepares you for Step Four, lifelong change!

Change happens in the moment. It is an instantaneous event that can occur in any step of the UnlimitedGrowth process. You may never know exactly when the change occurred; however, you will know you are different.

Change happens by intervening at one of two places on the wheel of belief we discussed earlier. Change occurs by replacing an old belief with a new, more constructive belief or by emphatically deciding to be different. Because it is easy to fool ourselves into thinking we have changed simply because we made a decision to be different, I have chosen to structure this book around change occurring at the point of belief rather than decision.

The first three steps of UnlimitedGrowth prepare your conscious, subconscious, and unconscious minds for permanent change!

Although there are many successful tools to facilitate lasting change, I have chosen to focus on Meditation 2 in the Meditation Appendix, called Changing Your Beliefs.

Use this meditation as often as you want. As we have discussed, meditations work when you allow yourself to experience your feelings to the fullest extent. In using this meditation, it is important to feel your desire to change, to imagine how life will be once you have changed, and to expect the change to occur. Hold these feelings during the entire meditation and enhance them as you actually change the belief in the meditation.

When you start out, change only one belief per meditation. As you progress and become more proficient, you can eventually change up to three beliefs with each process, providing they pertain to the same topic. For instance, you can change three beliefs based on love. At another time, you can change some beliefs pertaining to men or to women. However, you should not mix topics and try to change a belief about men or women and romantic relationships in the same meditation.

Homegrowth 6: Changing Your Beliefs

Complete Meditation 2, Changing Your Beliefs, located in the Meditation Appendix.

With this final meditation, you will have completed all four steps of UnlimitedGrowth:

1. Notice
2. Acknowledge
3. Forgive
4. Change!

Homegrowth 7: Life After Change— Enhancing New Beliefs

(1) When you have successfully changed a belief by completing all four steps of UnlimitedGrowth, reinforce your new belief by repeating Meditation 2, Changing Your Beliefs, two or three more times.

(2) Instead of writing the new belief, reread it.

(3) As you read your new belief, actually *feel* what it is like to have that belief as part of your life.

→ Picture how your life will be different.

→ Expect your life to be the best you have ever imagined.

Ready Reference

This chapter can be used as an easy reference to changing your beliefs in the future. Once you have worked the entire UnlimitedGrowth process, the steps become easier. The time you spend in processing will be reduced because you are familiar with the steps. Your energy will be more appropriately focused on your feelings and your beliefs instead of on learning the process.

Change and growth are not guaranteed by time spent; they are assured by your desire to change, your ability to imagine yourself changed, and the expectation that you will indeed be different.

Lifelong Lessons

In Our End Is Our Beginning

We have come full circle. Initially, we began by searching for the perfect relationship, the ultimate woman or man who would make our lives complete. However, our search has led, not to the perfect man or woman, but to a more complete relationship with ourselves.

Our search brought us to the discovery of two very important life lessons:

1. Our beliefs create our reality.
2. We have in our lives what we really want.

These life lessons have enabled us to begin a long-awaited journey inward.

So far on this journey, we have discovered the power in our beliefs. We have climbed a spiraling path as we learned how our beliefs dictate our experiences. Our experiences, in turn, honor our beliefs, thus allowing us to create a new reality based on what we truly want. We have learned it is essential to know what we believe and to understand how our beliefs are manifested on a daily basis.

From now on, our journey knows no limits. This book also contains fascinating side trips that will allow us to continue to gather skills and tools useful in creating and re-creating our realities in an ever-flowing, conscious celebration of life.

Moving On

As I reviewed what I had learned, I found I had a new energy for creating my life more consciously than ever before. As

I gained a deeper knowledge of myself, I was able to use the new information as an ally. Becoming conscious of the beliefs that create my reality returned the power of my life and my experiences to me . . . where it naturally resides. Learning how to change the beliefs that no longer serve me has allowed me to continually create a reality based upon personal power.

Finally I was ready to explore the greatest love of all.

Chapter Three
Reclaiming the Power

We Are Love

Somewhere hidden in the depths of all humankind is the knowledge that life itself is based on love. But sometimes, behind our veiled awareness, we have difficulty seeing love in ourselves or in anyone else. We forget how it feels to hold a baby against our naked skin, or how the cool morning dew tingles our toes as we greet the new day. We ignore the wonder of a child's uninhibited joy and the magic of an evening fire. Instead of experiencing all the joys, we hide from ourselves and deny our true inner essence — *love!*

We wander, lost in darkness, until we discover someone we hope will bring light into our world. We ignore the fact that this special someone simply mirrors our own essence of love. We are the source and bearers of our own light. That spark of light we see reflected in those we love is based on our willingness to be what we truly are — love. When we are loving, we are simply practicing the art of being ourselves.

I have often wondered why we don't talk about our lovingness more. We talk about wanting to be *in* love and *falling* in love. We talk about sex and our sexual activities, but we rarely talk about actual *loving*. Perhaps now is the time to allow ourselves to talk about and thus experience our own love.

Life's Greatest Lesson

The most important lesson we will ever learn is to love ourselves. Yet how many of us have actually been taught how to do that?

It seems to me that for most of our lives, people teach us how *not* to love ourselves. We are taught to judge ourselves, to be self-critical, and to find ourselves lacking. There is no doubt in my mind we all could tell horrendous stories about our childhoods.

The truth is, most of us have had sorrowful experiences in our pasts, yet we continue to hang onto these unhappy memories as if they were red badges of courage. As adults, we continue to use them to dictate our feelings and actions. More important, we continue to define our current love experiences by these outdated memories of childhood.

Learning Love?

Children learn about love from their parents. However, if our parents did not love themselves, how could they possibly teach us to love ourselves? Instead, they taught us what they knew—how *not* to love ourselves.

Our parents and teachers, overtly and covertly, taught us that love must be earned. From the very beginning, we learned to search for love from outside sources instead of developing the essence of love within ourselves. It is indeed unfortunate that our culture has sadly neglected teaching our children to love and honor themselves.

However, you and I are no longer children, and it is no longer appropriate or healthy for us to act on childhood memories. When we learn not to respond to situations based on childhood experiences, we can begin to love ourselves as adults. Letting go of the past will allow us to experience the essence of self-love in ways that honor us now, today.

Step Two of UnlimitedGrowth: Acknowledge

My relationship with Jonathan was drowning in the past, but I could not see it. However, I did notice feeling lonely. The more I thought about it, the more I realized I felt lonely all the time. "Lonely" had become my natural way of being.

Walking the path of my memories, I was astonished to discover I had felt lonely throughout my childhood. I was so accustomed to feeling lonely, I had not consciously identified it in a long while.

Recognizing I had a feeling I did not want, coupled with behavior predicated upon that feeling, I moved to the first step of UnlimitedGrowth, Notice.

Noticing meant I could decide to keep the feeling and consequent behavior or I could move to the second step of UnlimitedGrowth, Acknowledge.

It did not take me long to decide I wanted to change my pervasive loneliness and its repercussions. I was no longer willing to act in the present as I always had in the past. This decision led to the second step of UnlimitedGrowth.

As outlined in Chapter 2, *acknowledging* is a two-phase process:

1. You gain an *understanding* of why you created and maintained a belief or feeling that does not work for you.
2. You accept responsibility for the *impact* this feeling has on yourself and others.

The first phase of acknowledging involves discovering the hidden motives behind the belief, feeling, or behavior you want to change. You can find those hidden motives by learning about your emotional payoffs.

Understanding

At some time or another, each of us has realized we persist in feelings or behavior that are destructive to us. We know it, we see it clearly, we even promise ourselves to change, yet we continue to repeat the same pattern. Why?

The answers to this question are varied and intricate. You and I continue patterns that do not work for us because we receive some kind of benefit, some emotional payoff, for our feelings or behavior. Discovering our payoffs is a vital step toward understanding why we feel and behave as we do. It is also an important step toward accepting responsibility for the impact we have on ourselves and others.

When I recognized my current loneliness was left over from my childhood, I wanted to release it. However, until I learned *why* I chose to live with loneliness for so long, until I understood what my payoffs were, I could not change my feeling.

Payoff Questions*

The following questions helped me discover exactly what my payoffs were for hanging on to my loneliness. These Payoff Questions allowed me to take a deeper look within myself. They can be used for *any* behavior, thought, feeling, or belief you would like to change. The goal of these questions is to awaken your consciousness to the motives behind your behavior. When you answer these questions honestly, you can eliminate the possibility of using your subconscious mind as an excuse for feelings and behavior that hurt you or others.

*Lazaris, *New Dynamics of Processing and Programming,* © 1989 NPN Publishing, Inc.

Your feelings and behaviors then become conscious choices for which you are responsible.

Since it will be important to use these questions on a regular basis, each question is assigned a key word for easy recall.

Key Word: *Avoid*

What am I trying to avoid by maintaining my current behavior?

This question can be answered by exploring what feelings we are trying *not* to feel and what actions we try *not* to make.

When we think of the word *avoid*, we usually think of emotions we label negative, such as hurt, hate, anger, jealousy. Yet we often try to avoid positive feelings such as success, love, and responsibility as well. Any time our behavior eliminates any form of goodness from our lives, we are actually avoiding the full spectrum of our feelings. For example, if we consistently fail in our relationships, perhaps we want to avoid the positive feelings of intimacy, love, and happiness.

Key Word: *Righteousness*

What righteous feelings am I hanging onto?

This question helps us explore feelings we think we have earned the right to feel. We often use these righteous feelings as a shield to protect us from further hurt. The trouble is, it doesn't work. For example, we might feel we have been hurt by men or women and therefore we have a right to be angry. This question asks us to explore feelings we have justified because of our past experiences.

Any time we add righteousness to a feeling, we eliminate the possibility of releasing the feeling because righteousness is like superglue. It keeps us stuck in a feeling for as long as we insist, "I have the *right* to feel as I do!" Although the feeling has become destructive or outdated, it still is stuck.

Key Word: *Blame*

Who am I trying to blame—either out of misguided love or the desire to punish—for my current behavior?

Many times, we continue unhealthy behavior because we are trying to punish or show love for others. At the time, we may not notice we are actually blaming those we want to punish—or love—for our circumstances.

For example, Pete's mother really wanted him to get married and he was sick to death of what his mother wanted. Out of anger, he destroyed his romantic relationships so he would never have to get married. In short, his behavior—not maintaining a relationship—was his way of punishing his mother.

On the other hand, Jane found herself in a position of making more money than her father ever dreamed of. She had been in this position before, yet just when things looked wonderful, they fell apart. Perhaps she created the failure out of misguided love for her father. She did not want to hurt him by achieving more than he did. Though her original goal was to honor her love for her father, she ended up blaming him for her career failures.

The question of who we are trying to blame will help us find our camouflaged excuses for not creating what we say we want. At first the answers might not be obvious. However, our behavior can give us insight into motivations that are deeper than we usually look. We are looking for the people or situations we blame—consciously or unconsciously.

Key Word: *Guarantee*

What guarantee do I want before I will be willing to change?

A guarantee might sound something like this: "Before I agree to be really vulnerable in this relationship, I want God to promise I'll never be hurt." Or: "Before I really put effort into getting the job I want, I must know I am going to get it." Since guarantees illuminate our secret fears, this question helps us discover them. In the first example, by demanding a guarantee that we will not be hurt, we expose our fear that we will. In the second example, our fear of failure or of not being enough is uncovered by demanding a guarantee of success.

Key Word: *Self-Pity*

How much pleasure do I get from self-pity?

For many, self-pity is obvious. We walk around complaining about how bad life is. We believe we are victims of bad luck, unfortunate circumstances, or mean people. For some of us, this hanged-dog kind of self-pity is too overt. We are more subtle. Yet the very nature of our subtlety deludes us into believing we are not indulging in self-pity.

Before skipping this Payoff Question, as not applicable to you, take a second look. Self-pity also manifests as frustration or anger at things that never go quite right. For example, we might feel sorry for ourselves because we have no friends who add positively to our lives. In this question, explore the more subtle "poor me's." (See the Bibliography, which lists books and tapes on the subtleties and dangers of self-pity.)

Key Word: *Self-Importance*

How does my behavior make me feel better than other people?

"My case is special. I have suffered for so long that I could not possibly use techniques and information that work for others. I need special attention and special exercises just for me." This I-have-it-so-bad scenario is only one side of the self-importance coin. Notice how being "the worst" at something can make us feel as arrogant as being "the best."

Self-importance can also sound like this: "Listen, I'm not as crippled as the women/men I read about. I have my act together. There is really nothing anyone can tell me about my life that I do not already know." Another aspect of this side of the coin involves feelings of importance based on the circumstances of birth, geographic location, or financial status.

Key Word: *The Past*

Why am I clinging to the past?

Some of us hold on to our old ways simply because we are not willing to do the work required to move ahead. Others of us are afraid to move out of the past because we lack the skills required to handle life situations in new and different ways.

Still others of us have no intention of even considering change because, somewhere within us, we know that if we change we will have to give up manipulation, domination, and self-centered behavior.

Finally, many of us remain stuck in the past because we fear the unknown, not knowing if we will be able to cope with the future.

Homegrowth 8: Exploring the Why

(1) List ten feelings or behaviors you would like to change.

EXAMPLE:
When I have a lover in my life, I give up my activities and devote all of my time to him or her.

---

(2) Choose one item from your list and write your answers for all of the Payoff Questions listed below.

→ You will find it more beneficial to write these questions in the form of self-dialogue rather than as short-sentence or one-word answers.

Avoid: What am I trying to avoid by maintaining my current behavior?

Righteousness: What righteous feelings am I hanging onto?

Blame: Who am I trying to blame—either out of misguided love or the desire to punish—for my current behavior?

Guarantee: What guarantee do I want before I will be willing to change?

Self-Pity: How much pleasure do I get from self-pity?

Self-Importance: How does my behavior make me feel better than other people?

The Past: Why am I clinging to the past?

As you use these Payoff Questions repeatedly, you may discover you use two or three payoffs more frequently than others. Sometimes all seven may be germane to the issue, while other times, only a few will be. As you become familiar with your payoffs, you will be able to identify your unique pattern.

Recognizing our payoffs leads to a deeper understanding of our beliefs, feelings, and behavior. *Understanding* is the first phase in the second step of UnlimitedGrowth.

This new understanding allows us to take responsibility for our *impact* on ourselves and others, the second phase in Step Two of UnlimitedGrowth. Before we can take responsibility for our impact, let's investigate what impact is.

Impact

Impact is the effect our beliefs, feelings, and behaviors have on the world around us. Because we have an innate desire to bond, we have agreed to have impact on others and to be impacted upon by others.

Self-honoring beliefs, feelings, and behaviors are rarely harmful to others. However, impact caused by the beliefs, feelings, and behaviors that damage us also injures those we care about.

It is important to consider both ourselves and those we care about when examining our negative impact. At the beginning of this chapter, I mentioned that most of us never learned to love ourselves. We never learned to honor ourselves as the most precious commodity in our lives. Hence we continue in self-destructive behavior, wallowing in self-pity, and believing we are never good enough. We alone are responsible for this negative impact in our lives. When we take this responsibility, we take one more step toward changing those old patterns—one more step in UnlimitedGrowth.

Perhaps the more important aspect of impact is accepting responsibility for the negative impact we have on those we care about. Accepting this responsibility is the clearest way to perceive the power of impact. Sometimes realizing just how destructive we are to those we love can motivate us to do the work necessary to change.

When we take responsibility for the negative impact we have on those around us, we focus on the emotional damage we cause. We seek out and discover our "uglies"—the hurtful manipulations, dominations, and controls that are part of our daily lives. For some of us, seeing our negative impact will be obvious. Others of us, whose "uglies" are camouflaged in subtle maneuverings, will have to search more diligently.

Homegrowth 9: Impact and Responsibility

(1) Review the seven Payoff Questions you have just completed in Homegrowth 8, Exploring the Why.

(2) Using the work you completed in Homegrowth 8, write about the impact each payoff has had on you. Go into as much detail as possible.

EXAMPLE:
Avoid (impact on myself):
- By avoiding relationships, I am depriving myself of happiness.

(3) Write about the impact each payoff has had on the other people in your life. You will want to take the time to think about your impact and write all your feelings in detail. Ask yourself:

- What was my hurtful behavior?
- How did my behavior affect the other person?
- Why did I want to hurt him or her?

EXAMPLE:
Avoid (impact on others):
- Because I am unhappy, I am often short-tempered and snap at my friend.
- My behavior is hurtful both to my friend and to our relationship.

UnlimitedGrowth: Work Completed

1. *Notice* what feelings or behaviors you wanted to change.
2. *Acknowledge.*
   a. *Understand* why you behave as you do by learning about your payoffs.
   b. Accept responsibility for your *impact* on yourself and others.

Payoff Antidotes

Now that you know your payoffs and have accepted responsibility for their impact, you have the power to do something about them. In order to defuse the payoffs, you can learn to alter your responses to them. By choosing a response that will counteract the effects of your self-destructive behavior, you can detoxify your payoffs.

For each payoff, there is an antidote that can help you respond differently and move us out of unhealthy feelings and behaviors. The key words for the antidotes are identical to those of the payoffs.

Antidote for *Avoid*

Tell yourself the truth.

By honestly facing the issues we previously sidestepped, we can detoxify this payoff. For instance, if I have discovered I am avoiding the happiness inherent in a romantic relationship, I need to consider why I fear happiness. If I can tell myself the truth, "I'm afraid of happiness," I can then deal with the fear and move on.

Antidote for *Righteousness*

Let go of the hurt and anger.

Since most of our righteousness centers around feelings of hurt and anger, we can learn to let go of these feelings. When we decide not to punish others for what they have done to us, we can release the weapon of righteousness.

Antidote for *Blame*

1. Process your feelings.
2. Accept responsibility.

By acknowledging and processing the feelings that produced the blame, we begin to clear blame. Then, as we take responsibility for the events we create in our lives, we can defuse blame's toxicity.

Antidote for *Guarantee*

Accept total responsibility.

Accepting responsibility for absolutely everything we create in our lives is the antidote for needing a guarantee before we will risk. By taking total responsibility for creating our lives, we can evaluate our choices more consciously. When we know we are responsible for everything that happens in our lives, it is easier to make choices and decisions that honor us. When we make decisions that honor us, we no longer need a guarantee from the Universe. Our self-honoring decisions are our guarantee.

Antidote for *Self-Pity*

Ask for and receive help.

To end self-pity, sincerely ask for help and utilize it when it is extended. It is impossible to feel sorry for ourselves when we are asking for and receiving help.

Antidote for *Self-Importance*

Develop self-intimacy.

Since self-importance stems from feelings of inadequacy, the antidote is to become intimate with yourself. Spend time getting to know yourself; learn to recognize your value. Working through this book is an excellent step in the pursuit of self-intimacy.

Antidote for *the Past*

Let go of old patterns.

The way to let go of the past is to explore, identify, and change old feelings and patterns that no longer serve us. It is also important to stay current with our present feelings. (For detailed information on processing feelings, refer to the Bibliography in the subsections on Success, Feelings, and Healing Abuse.)

Step Three of UnlimitedGrowth: Forgive

Now that we have explored the first two steps of Unlimited-Growth, we can move on to the third step, Forgive.

Frequently, we try to get others to forgive us and often they do. Yet, we still don't feel free or unburdened. Why? Because we have forgotten self-forgiveness.

There are three basic types of forgiveness. First, there is universal forgiveness, which entails asking to be forgiven by whatever God we believe in. Second, there is forgiveness for and from other human beings. Last—and most critically—there is self-forgiveness.

Universal Forgiveness

I began to learn about the process of forgiveness while I was in training to become a psychotherapist. I had a profound and unforgettable experience of universal forgiveness. In graduate school, we learned group therapy by participating in our own group sessions during class. One memorable session erupted into a life-changing experience for me.

"My father died when I was twelve," I told the group, but I looked directly into my instructor's eyes as if the others were nonexistent. "I was sad, and I was glad."

"Tell us about the glad part," my instructor gently prodded.

"If he was dead, then I didn't have to worry about him hurting anyone." I felt the familiar constriction in my chest as tears began to cloud my vision. "He used to come home drunk and beat up on my mom." Fifteen years later, and the pain still lived within me as raw and cutting as shredded glass on bare feet. The group sat quietly and waited while I cried.

The words came, the words that surprised and overwhelmed me. "I killed him. You see that don't you, I killed him. I wished that he was dead for so long, he finally just died."

"How did you kill him, Kimberley?" Again, my instructor asked his question with care and concern.

I was terrified as the answer came spilling forth. "In the front hall," I said through my sobs. "I hit him over the head with my judo trophy. I hit him and hit him and hit him. I crushed his head." I wanted to jump up and run, I wanted to stay. I didn't know what to do.

"Kimberley." The compassionate voice held me in place. "Kimberley, is he dead?"

"Yes!" The voice of a little girl came from my throat. "And he won't hurt my mom anymore." I clasped my knees with my arms, pulling myself into a tight ball.

The part of my mind that always watches couldn't believe what was happening. The wounded child within me was finally getting an opportunity to express her fear and hate. As many times as I, an adult woman, had worked through my hate for my father, I had never experienced it at such a deep level.

Now, as I sat huddled in my protective ball, I cried. I cried for the lost little girl in me that wanted a daddy to love and hold her, and yet I knew that could never be. I cried for the woman I had become—isolated and nontrusting. But most of all, I cried with relief. I had finally discovered the unfaced secret. The terrible thing I had held against myself all these years was my father's death. Now, I knew!

That little girl, that child within me, had spent so many nights waiting up for her father to come home, wondering what she would do if he hurt her mom one more time. Eventually, that innocent child convinced herself she actually had killed her father.

At the age of twelve, I had thought it out carefully: If he hit my mom just once more, I would go downstairs with my heavy judo trophy and hit him over the head. He would be dead. The thought was there, implanted in my brain.

Then one day, my father didn't come home; he had been blown up in a boating accident. The thought in my brain became reality—a reality I stuffed so deep within me, I didn't even know it was there. My thinking mind knew I had nothing to do with my father's death, but the little girl inside me had branded my soul.

Ask and It Shall Be Forgiven

After my tears were spent, my instructor said, "Gently, close your eyes. Answer this question silently to yourself: What would have to happen in order for you to know you were forgiven for your father's death?"

An image began to form in my mind as I sat with my head buried in my knees listening to the calming voice of my instructor. In this image, I was kneeling at the top of a hill looking up into the eyes of one who was suffering, too. At the same moment I looked up at Him, He opened His eyes and smiled down at me from the cross. At that instant, I connected with all the goodness of the Universe and was one with it. I knew I had been forgiven, and I cried with joy.

Because of my particular religious background, the scene I saw was appropriate for me. You might see a totally different picture. The scene is not what matters. What matters is the feeling.

Forgiving Others: The Next Step Toward Independence

This experience was so profound I thought I was finished once and for all with the pain. I was wrong. I just did not know it. As I continued to move through my life learning and growing, I noticed many areas of my life were still out of sync, and I wondered why. If I knew God had forgiven me, then why was I still so angry? Was there more to this forgiveness stuff than I had first thought?

I soon learned it was not enough to be forgiven by the force I now call God/Goddess/All That Is. I needed to take a much more difficult step; I needed to forgive my father. I tried every way I knew to deny this need. My father had forsaken me; he was never around when I needed him; he had hurt the people I loved; and, worst of all, I believed he had never loved me.

The little girl inside me was angry, and forgiveness did not play a part in her anger. Until I learned about forgiveness, I had never realized how my anger at people who have hurt me kept me from happiness. By not forgiving my father, *I* was inflicting pain upon myself, more than *he* ever could.

When we refuse to forgive someone, it is ourselves we hold hostage, not the person we refuse to forgive. Locking ourselves within walls of hate, we stubbornly stand guard. The price of freedom is forgiveness.

This was neither a quick nor an easy lesson for me. In fact, it was nearly four years after I learned about universal forgiveness that I began to work on forgiving my father. I discovered I could forgive him in phases. In the first phase, I had to discover and forgive the *why*—the reasons behind his behavior. In the second phase, I would have to forgive the behavior itself, the *what*.

I knew if I were to forgive my father, I would have to learn more about him. What I discovered about his history allowed me to understand the abused, raging child within him. Only then could I develop compassion for the child he once was. This new knowledge, understanding, and compassion prepared me to forgive the why. I could forgive why my father had become subhuman and abused his family.

Forgiving the why did not excuse his behavior. Nor did it justify the pain and scarring he caused. But it was a way for me to begin to forgive and let go.

Forgiving those who abuse us is often a difficult and painful process. But understanding can make it easier to forgive the reasons they were abusive. Forgiving the *why* is the first phase in forgiving others.

When we forgive the *why*, we can open the door to forgive the *what*. What my father did scarred and hurt me. Not forgiving continues the hurt. When I was ready to give up the hurt and move on, I could forgive the what. But I was not ready to forgive the what until I had healed the hurt.

Homegrowth 10: Forgiving Others

(1) Bring to mind someone you have not yet forgiven. When you are ready, use Meditation 1, Finally Free, from the Meditation Appendix. Adapt the meditation by replacing ugly you with the one you have come to forgive.

(2) You might do the meditation several times to forgive the *whys* of the behavior that hurt you. You will know how many times you need to do the meditation by monitoring your feelings.

(3) In your own timing, use the adapted meditation again to forgive the *what*—the actual behavior that hurt you.

Self-Forgiveness: Releasing the Final Bond

After I had forgiven my father, I was finally free—or so I thought.

As the years passed, and I continued to grow, occasionally I would notice pangs of pain when I remembered my father. Though I thought I had cleaned the closet of this skeleton, I had merely moved it from one hook to another.

I had been forgiven by the Universe, and I had forgiven my father. If forgiveness was the answer to a happier life, why wasn't I able to throw that old skeleton out and be more loving to myself? I finally realized I had left out a very important kind of forgiveness.

True, it is important that we feel forgiven by God/Goddess/All That Is, just as it is important that we forgive others. Yet the closet is not totally cleared until we can forgive ourselves. This is why self-forgiveness is the third step in UnlimitedGrowth. Until we forgive ourselves, it is unlikely that we will truly change.

Self-forgiveness is the ability to let go of the feelings of self-condemnation and self-anger. Self-forgiveness is a powerful act of loving-kindness. When we forgive ourselves, we let go of the self-condemning parts of our pasts, allowing us the freedom to embrace a more loving future.

Homegrowth 11:
Self-Forgiveness: Finally Free

(1) Review the work you completed in Homegrowth 9, Impact and Responsibility.

(2) Choose one of the hurtful behaviors you have identified.

(3) Decide to forgive yourself for your hurtful behavior.

→ If you are not yet ready to forgive yourself for what you did, forgive yourself for *why* you did it.

(4) Complete the Meditation 1, Finally Free, found in the Meditation Appendix.

→ This meditation should leave you feeling lighter, freer, and more at peace. It is geared to communicate with both your conscious and subconscious minds, thus allowing self-forgiveness to be more complete.

(5) Repeat this meditation until your heart and your gut tell you that you have truly forgiven yourself.

→ Even if you do none of the other exercises in this book, this one Homegrowth exercise can change your life. This is the power of self-forgiveness.

The Secret Self

The most insidious aspect of our feelings of self-condemnation and self-anger is that we do not always know where they come from.

While we were learning to "do good" and be who our parents and society wanted us to be, we also learned to hide the things *they* thought were "bad."

Eventually, we began to believe the "bad" things they thought about us were actually true. So we began to hide these "bad" or "ugly" things even from ourselves. These hidden beliefs, thoughts, feelings, and behaviors became our deep, dark secrets, causing feelings of fear, anger, and hurt. The worst part is we no longer remember why we have these feelings.

For example, I am amazed at the number of adults in therapy today who have recently discovered they were sexually abused when they were children. They carried around feelings of fear, anger, shame, and hurt without knowing the origin of these emotions until they began to explore them in therapy.

Discovering these secrets on our own can be frightening; however, therapy can often provide a safe environment where we can explore our hidden secrets. When we begin to explore our seemingly inexplicable feelings of fear, anger, and hurt, we begin to rediscover the secrets we have kept so well.

Can You Keep a Secret?

More readily dealt with than the secrets we have kept from ourselves are those we have kept from others. Once these are cleared away, they no longer block our access to what lies below them—the secrets we have kept hidden from ourselves.

The following Homegrowth is designed to help you clear away the secrets you have immediate access to, the secrets you have kept from the other people in your life.

Homegrowth 12: Into the Light

As with all Homegrowths, Into the Light is confidential, just for you alone. In fact, when you complete this exercise, destroy it if you wish.

(1) On a sheet of paper, which you can destroy later if you wish, write about the things you hope no one ever discovers about you, the secrets you hold deep within.

(2) Write what you are afraid will happen if anyone discovers your secrets.

(3) Write why these have become secrets, asking yourself these questions:

- What feelings do I want to hide?
- How am I blaming myself for what happened?
- What do I maintain is true about me because this happened?
- Who else was involved and what was that person's responsibility?

(4) Investigate and discover why you did what you did.

(5) Do Meditation 1, Finally Free, found in the Meditation Appendix, for each secret you have not already forgiven. If you cannot yet forgive the behavior, start with forgiving the *why* of the behavior.

Failure: Another Road to Freedom

Another way to explore self-forgiveness is to notice our attitudes about ourselves and the world around us. For example, our attitudes about failure can tell us how to be more forgiving of ourselves.

Traditionally, failure means "not enough." Somehow we have not been enough, and so we are a failure. It does not even matter what we failed. More than failure, it is this pervasive, self-critical attitude that is harmful.

I believe there is a different, more positive way to perceive failure. A personal failure of my own compelled me to explore some new ways of looking at "failure."

My first "real" job as a physician's assistant (P.A.) was with a large health maintenance organization in California. I was hired, as many P.A.s are, to assume the general duties of a family practitioner. What made this my dream job, however, was the opportunity to use my psychiatric training.

Leaving friends and family behind, I headed West to the Promised Land, alone, excited, and painfully naïve.

After four months on my dream job, I was unceremoniously asked to tender my resignation. My brain went into a haze similar to the smog that permanently shrouded L.A. I did not even ask why I was fired. I had failed, I had been sacked from my first job as a P.A., and I did not even know why.

I closed my office door, slumped into my new leather chair, and cried. In fact, I spent the better part of the next two days crying. I was immobilized with fear. What would happen to me in this strange place so far from home, with no family or friends?

Finally, when both my dog and cat were so fed up with my tears that they would not even look at me, I pulled myself together. In those days, I had not yet learned about payoffs, but I did know I was responsible to move out of my self-pity. I also knew I was the only one around to take care of me; I was the only one who could make my life work. I finally remembered that I had a lot to offer. I would find someone who needed my talents as badly as I wanted to share them.

In less than a week, I found an excellent job that catapulted me into a new life. This job demanded I expand, stretch, and grow beyond the bounds of traditional psychiatry and medicine.

Being fired was the first step on a long road to a new kind of freedom. Failing allowed me the freedom to take a clearer, less restrictive view of my life. It gave me an opportunity to look closely at myself and what I wanted, not what I thought I should want.

Failure was not the most elegant way to learn, but I took advantage of the opportunity it afforded me. That was the key: I learned to take advantage of whatever I created. Being willing to utilize the opportunities failure granted me was an act of self-forgiveness.

Now, when I "fail," I search for the hidden gifts. If we perceive our failures as doorways to continued growth and freedom, our lives will be spent seeking the hidden gifts instead of mourning what we did not create.

Although we may not like it, the truth is we do fail. But as long as we create a life that includes failure, we may as well reap some benefits. Perceiving our failures as gifts allows us to view ourselves from a new perspective.

Homegrowth 13:
The Hidden Gifts of Failure

(1) List the major failures in your life, each on a separate piece of paper.

EXAMPLE:
- A failed relationship

---

(2) In retrospect, what did you gain from each failure? Write your response on the corresponding page listing that failure.

(3) Make a list of questions to help you realize why you failed. Write these below your previous response.

EXAMPLE:
- Do I really want a relationship?
- What would my life be like without a partner?
- What advantages are there in independence?

There can be a time in our lives when we learn without failure. There can be a time when we discover and learn about ourselves because it is fun to do so. But until that time, the most self-forgiving act is to perceive our failures as opportunities to grow.

We have traveled a long way in this chapter, laying much of the necessary groundwork we will need for permanent change and personal growth. Most important, we have completed the first three steps of UnlimitedGrowth:

1. *Notice* which beliefs, feelings, and behaviors no longer serve us, including

   • those that are harmful and
   • those we choose to change.

2. *Acknowledge* encompasses two phases:

   a. *understanding* why we participate in such behavior,
   b. accepting responsibility for the *impact* this behavior has on our lives as well as the lives of others.

We learned to recognize exactly what our payoffs are and how they keep us locked into toxic behavior. We also learned the antidotes to those payoffs, allowing ourselves to take another step in UnlimitedGrowth, closer to permanent change.

3. *Self-forgiveness*, the third step in UnlimitedGrowth, releases us from the bondage of the hurts that have happened in our lives. This step is so powerful that even when taken by itself, it can change our lives immediately.

In Chapter Four, we will delve into the true essence of love and its impact on our lives.

Chapter Four
And What Is Love?

Have you ever wondered why no one ever taught us the really important stuff? I do not mean the "junk" that was jackhammered into our heads, allegedly to make us "well-rounded" human beings. I mean the really good stuff—like sex, boys and girls, death, birth, and *magic*—like *love*.

Haven't you ever wondered why someone, somewhere, didn't teach us about love?

To Each Generation
Its Lesson—and Its Truth

Each generation, in its own way, has added markedly to our culture. Each has left a legacy for the following generation to build upon. Therefore, if previous generations have not taught us about love, perhaps it is because they did not know much about it.

Some may argue we were not taught about love because it is not something that needs teaching; it is a given, a known factor which is too obvious to contemplate. I, however, disagree. I believe we were not taught about love because love simply was not the foremost concern of previous generations.

At the beginning of the twentieth century, people often married for reasons of survival rather than love. They married to make their parents' load a bit easier by eliminating a mouth to feed. Or they married to provide extra hands to make homes and farms function more adequately. They married in order to survive, and, thus, marriage meant security. We imagine the days of prearranged marriages and selling off daughters as part of ancient history, but in times when marriage was necessary for survival, love was simply not a prerequisite.

The lesson of that turn-of-the-century generation was to secure its survival by creating a system of social mores—a culture. The basis of this culture was marriage and family. Neither was created for or from love.

During the 1930s, many people continued to marry because it was the mutually agreed upon way of life. Without questioning why, children grew up, got married, and had more children. When the Great Depression was in full swing, combining forces insured survival of the individual as well as the culture. Love? Who had time?

During World War II, survival of the culture became synonymous with survival of humankind. The legacy of this generation was to guarantee the survival of the human race by adhering to the traditions of the culture.

Later, during the 1950s, basic day-to-day survival became less of an issue. However, social survival—living within preset cultural standards—became a priority. As we have discussed, while the previous generations struggled with economic and political survival, they created a cultural network of intricate social mores that became more pervasive than the basic issue of survival itself. Honoring this cultural network became the lesson of the 1950s generation.

Though the members of this postwar generation were certainly caught in the social styles of "women's roles," "male responsibility," and "duty," they began to yearn for more of everything in their lives, including more meaningful, loving marriages. This was the pivotal generation. Since survival was basically assured, they began to focus on the *quality* of their lives.

The preceding history is an oversimplified generalization of our economic, political, and social evolution, yet the point is each generation has its own unique lesson and thus new wisdom to leave future generations. However, it is the responsibility of the current generation to decide what wisdom and truth to follow, and what to discard and leave behind.

Because the postwar generation moved beyond survival, today's generation is faced with an unprecedented opportunity. Because we no longer spend all our time and energy on basic survival needs, we can probe, explore, and question our cultural, emotional, and spiritual needs. And because we are more able to assess and meet our new needs, we yearn even more keenly for connected, loving relationships.

As we search for these new loving relationships, we are giving ourselves permission to explore the intricacies of these relationships. Perhaps it will be our generation's lesson to teach our children all about love. Perhaps it will be up to us to answer that eternal question: And what is love?

The Levels of Love

When I began to focus on my own cultural, emotional, and spiritual needs, I found myself in search of a better understanding of the phenomenon we call love. I remember trying to examine my feelings about Jonathan, but I simply did not comprehend much of what I was experiencing. If I did not even understand my feelings, how could I effectively deal with them?

My search led to a model of love that describes the seven levels of love.* These levels are Security Love, Sensual Love,

*Lazaris, "The Seven Levels of Love," Mill Valley, California.

Conditional Love, Unconditional Love, World Love, Universal Love, and Cosmic Love. Each is a step in our personal evolution. Each has its own characteristics and intricacies.

Because this book deals primarily with human relationships, I have chosen to discuss only the four levels that are readily understandable and accessible to most of us—Security Love, Sensual Love, Conditional Love, and Unconditional Love. In my perception, the last three levels of love—World Love, Universal Love, and Cosmic Love—provide us with a future goal, and perhaps the next generation's lesson.

Level One: Security Love

Security Love—the first level of love—stems primarily from our attempt to make the world safe. We can do this in one of two ways. We can attempt to get someone else to provide us with security, or we can provide it for ourselves.

It's Only an Illusion

For many of us, true security is another one of those intangibles, another illusion. We move from day to day in a world that continues to frighten us. And all too often, just when we think our world is infallibly safe (we have enough money, we have someone to love us, and so forth), the bottom falls out (we lose our job, our lover goes off with our best friend, etc.), and there we are, back where we started, frightened and alone.

Unfortunately, this process will continue as long as we convince ourselves that we alone cannot provide security for ourselves. We believe someone else must do it for us. We feel we must find a partner in order to make our world safe and secure.

Others of us know we can provide our own needs, but we refuse to do so because we want others to prove they love us by attempting to provide us with what we need. Our per-

ception of security becomes so distorted we absolutely refuse to be responsible for taking care of ourselves, for meeting our own needs.

There are several problems inherent in asking others to provide us with security. First, we must speculate on whether
someone can make our world safe. And second, we must be
presumptuous enough to think someone else will provide us
with security in a fashion satisfactory to us. The fact is, this
type of assumption and speculation can only lead to blame,
frustration, and hurt. However, far worse than the blame, frustration, and hurt are the messages we constantly give to ourselves when we ask others to make us feel safe. We are telling
ourselves we are not capable of taking care of ourselves, and
therefore we *need* someone else to do it for us.

The Child Within

The feeling of needing someone else to provide us with
security rings a resonant chord in most of us. Deep within,
we can feel the fear that provokes this neediness. It is cen-
tered in what many call "the child within."

The child within us is a very real and viable part of ourselves. It is much more than a psychological technique de-
vised to help us deal with our past pains. A product of frozen
development, the child within can be any age from birth to
age seven.

Somewhere in our pasts, we were hurt, betrayed, or mis-
handled. It does not matter if these feelings were caused
deliberately or by people who simply did not understand or
take responsibility for their impact. To a child, the feelings
are real, and decisions that dictate our entire lives are made
upon these feelings and perceptions.

Most of us believe we were not loved enough, and the child
within concurs. Now, as adults, it is up to us to access our
child within. We alone have the power to heal the child
within us. Until we do, the pain of childhood will bleed

through to every aspect of our lives—especially to our romantic relationships.

We are not always willing to admit we are acting on the insecurities of our child self. For example, asking a boyfriend to take your car to the mechanic because "mechanics relate better to men" or asking a girlfriend to pick out your clothes, or asking to borrow the rent money from dad because you were a little short this month could appear to be nothing more than innocent favors. Or they could be the cleverly disguised efforts of our child within to get others to make our world safer.

Some of us deny we ask our partners to provide us with security because our needs for security can be cleverly camouflaged. For some of us, just having a lover is security enough. For others, security is provided by the delusion that our partner's love will make us safe, and no one will ever be able to hurt us again.

Once we recognize that we ask others to provide our security, we can move away from the self-doubt of our child self. By meeting our own needs, we move into the true strength and security of our adult self.

The child within must be recognized and effectively healed. To help you deal with your child within and get on with the wonder of adulthood, I have listed several books and tapes in the Bibliography.

They Can't Do It for You

Even if it were possible for someone else to access our child, understand his or her needs, and attempt to provide his or her security, we would not allow it. Instinctively, we know that allowing someone else to provide the child within with security would jeopardize the growth we so desperately seek.

Human beings have a built-in fail-safe system where security is concerned. Somewhere inside, we know we must first take responsibility for ourselves. So even when we manage to maneuver another human being into taking responsibility for us, we automatically sabotage her or his efforts by judging those efforts not good enough. When we look to another to supply us with something that she or he cannot provide, the other always appears inadequate.

The strain we place on a relationship by asking another to provide what she or he cannot is unbearable. When we refuse to meet our own security needs, and insist that someone else do it for us, everyone loses. We end up feeling ripped off, angry, and cheated. In turn, the other person feels humiliated, angry, and not enough.

Security comes from within. Another human being does not have access to the frightened child who lives within us. We alone have the ability to reach and care for that fearful child who still hides under the darkened staircase. Only we can make it safe for the child within to come out and shine.

Security Means Self-Care

Because I have learned that others can not do it for me, the word *security* has taken on a new meaning for me. Now, at the mere mention of security, I automatically think of self-care. One way to become more secure is to become more caring of and for ourselves.

One of the best ways we can become more self-caring is to learn how to assess and meet our own needs. This is a vital step in our growth beyond the first level of love, Security Love, toward self-care. For without self-care, there can be no security.

Needs—What Are They?

Human beings have many different kinds of needs. Since most of us are familiar with our basic survival needs, let's take a closer look at our emotional needs. The following is my list of basic human emotional needs.

- We need to love and be loved.
- We need to connect, bond, and share with other human beings.
- We need to grow and stretch beyond what we know.
- We need to be challenged, to identify, and achieve our personal quest—to be more.
- We need to demonstrate self-trust, self-esteem, and self-confidence.
- We need to recognize, utilize, and honor our self-love, self-respect, and self-worth.
- We need to know that our very life makes a difference.
- We need to know we have impact; we need to know we matter.

In order to maintain a quality of life that honors our humanness, celebrates our uniqueness, and provides us with true security, I believe we first need to recognize our basic emotional needs. Second, we need to be willing to take responsibility for meeting these needs on a consistent basis. The quality of our lives varies depending on our willingness to recognize and meet our own individual needs.

Once we have honestly assessed and defined our needs, we are in a position to creatively meet those needs. However, if we are not clear about our needs, it becomes impossible to meet them successfully. Now would be an appropriate time to investigate and ascertain what your personal security needs are.

Homegrowth 14: Security Equals Self-Care

(1) To help organize and delineate your thoughts, use the following questions as guidelines to begin your investigation into your personal security needs.

- What are my physical security needs?
- How could my home be a safer place?

- Is my car or form of transportation located in a spot that is safe and secure?
- Have I familiarized myself with the basic points of physical safety available through a good self-defense course?
- Do my belief systems create a world of fear or do they create a world of peace?

(2) Look at the sentence completion in Homegrowth 3, You Are What You Believe, in Chapter Two. Following the same two-part format, complete the following sentences:

The world is _____ and I feel _____ .
Life is _____ and I feel _____ .

(3) Based on those exercises, make a list of beliefs you have identified as creating an unsafe reality for you.

(4) Finally, write your answers to the following questions:

- What emotional needs must I fulfill in order to feel secure?
- What emotional boundaries do I need to set in order to feel safe with my feelings and with the feelings of others?
- What do I need to do in order to give myself permission to safely express my feelings?

Taking Care of Our Own Needs

Once we have identified our needs, we can learn to fulfill them. We will never learn to trust ourselves unless we actually meet our own needs on a continuing basis.

One way to be gentle with ourselves during this process is to understand we do not have to do this alone. We can provide ourselves with good teachers. We can expose ourselves to new ideas and ways of perceiving life. We can stretch our awareness and challenge our beliefs and thoughts by reading books on goal setting and higher achievement, relationships, women, and men. (The Bibliography is a good place to begin.) Finally, we can surround ourselves with people who are authentic and willing to share of themselves and of their wisdom.

Meeting our needs on a consistent basis will return to us what we readily threw away—our security. When we constantly assess, evaluate, and meet our needs, our center of power remains where it belongs—with ourselves.

Needing to Need or Preferring to Need

Now that we have identified our needs and created ways to meet them, a new choice is available to us. We can *prefer* to need. There is a world of difference between preferring to need and needing to need. Needing to need is *expecting* someone else to take responsibility for our needs. We have these expectations because we honestly believe we cannot meet our own needs, or we want our needs met as proof we are loved.

Preferring to need can become an option only when we can acknowledge and meet our own needs on a consistent basis. Only then can we consciously choose to allow someone else to meet our needs.

Taking the Next Step

Now that we know it is impossible to place our security—or sense of safeness—in the hands of another, it becomes clear why a healthy adult relationship cannot sustain itself on the Security Level of love.

In my own situation with Jonathan, my fears reinforced my desire to have him meet my emotional needs, which in turn only drove him farther away.

As I plowed through my fears of needing Jonathan, an intricate shift occurred within me. When I no longer needed Jonathan to make my world secure, I could be more trusting, especially of myself. Learning to acknowledge and meet my own needs consistently allowed me to trust myself. Being more self-trusting enabled me to share myself more genuinely. And sharing myself with Jonathan in a more open and authentic way allowed us to reexperience a level of love we thought we knew all about—Sensual Love.

Level Two: Sensual Love

Sensual Love allows us to feast in the wonder of our senses and imagination. It is the level of love we sometimes think is most enjoyable because it is filled with romance, sex, and fantasy. This is the image of love we have learned to believe in. For many of us, Sensual Love is all we know of love.

Sensuality—Not Sexuality

Sensuality does not necessarily mean sex or sexuality. In other words, you can utilize your senses to create physical and emotional pleasure and not have—or even allude to—sex. This is often a difficult concept to understand because our sensual activities are usually planned with sex as the final goal. In short, sex, all too often, becomes the primary focus of our pleasure. We believe sex is the magic elixir of life, guaranteed to take care of all our aches, pains, and broken hearts.

Perhaps the following example best demonstrates how sensuality and sexuality can be totally different and yet be intertwined. Eating ice cream can be a very sensual experience. The texture, flavor, and temperature all lend themselves to sensuality. Savor the flavor of the ice cream, roll it around your mouth, and feel the ice flakes melt and slide off your tongue. Nibble at it, bite into it, or simply lick it.

All of the above are sensual experiences, yet none is necessarily sexual. However, all these experiences can become sexual by merely allowing your mind to fantasize about them. It is true, however, that sensuality and sexuality together can create *magic*. In Chapter Seven, we will explore how to create that kind of magical experience.

Sensuality, Our Pleasure Sense

Sensuality is what gives many of us our sense of being alive. We can feel it in the wind tearing at our clothing as it cascades over the ever-changing sand dunes when we walk along the beach. Sensuality is the scent of a lily or the touch of its velvety petals. Sensuality is the sound of children laughing, the cries of a lover's passion, or the harmony of notes woven together to form a symphony.

Sensual Love can be experienced when all of our senses are integrated. It is a unique blending of our physical, emotional, and psychological selves.

The Limits of Sensual Love

Sensual Love is, in and of itself, wonderful and magical. However, if we feel alive or truly connected with our partner only when we are relating at the sensual level, life itself becomes extremely limiting.

Sensuality added a spark to my relationship with Jonathan. It brought us closer and more in tune with each other. This bonding—this connecting of the senses—can be extremely powerful. Its wattage can give off so much heat and power we often find ourselves welded together in a relationship— sometimes happily, sometimes not.

The power of Sensual Love is undeniable, yet if it is the *only* thing that binds us, the weld will not secure the relationship over the stress of time. It will become rusted and its adhering power diminished.

Sensual Love helped Jonathan and me bond and expand our relationship. It also made me yearn for more. I wanted to continue to grow and connect more deeply. My desire led us to a greater understanding of the next level of love.

Level Three: Conditional Love

Conditional Love is love based upon our likes and dislikes. It boils down to just that. If you recall from my account in

Chapter One, the conditions I required in a man before I would consider him a viable partner were quite apparent. The fact is, if Jonathan had been fat and dumpy, I would never have noticed him getting out of his car, much less initiated a conversation with him.

Though it sounds shallow and superficial, Conditional Love only allows us to love and be loved if the other person meets our preconceived expectations of "someone I love." If the other person does not meet our conditions, we either pull away or push them away.

I'll Love You If . . .

In the process of being "culturalized" and socialized, we have all acquired prejudices and biases. When we were children, most of us were taught Conditional Love. We learned our "acceptability" or "right to be loved" was based upon our behavior and performance. Our parents had preconceived ideas about what their children should and should not be. We were pushed, pulled, and molded into what they thought we should be. When we attempted to pull free from their expectations, our behavior was met with rejection, punishment, or the withholding of love.

Not only have we carried our parents' biases with us into our adult years, we have picked up others along the way. Our notions of what is acceptable and not acceptable in a partner have been influenced by our teachers and the people we admired as adolescents, as well as our peers and the media. The fact is, everything that surrounds us—our entire environment—has expanded and intensified our prejudices, biases, and perceptions.

Because we are committed to personal growth, we can no longer act on these prejudices without consciously evaluating the impact they have on our lives and the lives of those we care about. Becoming honest about the conditions by which we judge the acceptability of our lovers is not always a pleasant realization. As I noticed my own conditions, I was painfully aware how superficial and trite I appeared, even to myself. However, it was also this painful awareness that helped me delete and revise some of the conditions I held.

The following Homegrowth will help you recognize your conditions and allow you the opportunity to change those that no longer serve you.

Homegrowth 15: What Condition Are Your Conditions in?

(1) On a piece of paper, prepare your personal "prerequisite" list for lovers.

→ List all the requirements another human being must have in order for you to enter into a romantic relationship with that person.

→ Since categories are helpful, you may want to include some of the following:

a. Physical Characteristics
   • height
   • hair style and color
   • body build
   • complexion

b. Economic Status
   • salary
   • debts
   • alimony/child support

c. Career Plans
   • upwardly mobile career
   • dislikes career
   • multiple jobs
   • self-employed
   • gives total priority to career

d. Social Status
 • divorced/separated
 • children
 • educational level
 • religion
 • ethnic background

e. Personality traits
 • demeanor
 • communicative/quiet
 • warm, loving, touching/aloof, reserved

This outline is certainly open-ended. Expand on it until the entire spectrum of your prerequisites are clearly delineated and defined.

(2) On a second piece of paper, list the characteristics in each category that are absolutely unacceptable in a lover.

(3) Review both lists.

(4) Now go back to the first list and put an "X" by the prerequisites you require in your *friends*.

(5) On list two, put an "X" by the characteristics you would not allow in a *friend*.

(6) As you review your separate lists, notice the differences. (In my experience, most of us are much more tolerant of our friends than of our lovers.)

Prejudices Versus Principles

The limits created by Conditional Love can be harmful to ourselves as well as the people around us. By its very nature, Conditional Love can cripple our ability to form intimate relationships. Clearly, Conditional Love, with its unconscious, culturally preprogrammed prejudices, is at least partially responsible for our feelings of unworthiness and "not enoughness."

However, while Conditional Love can reflect our petty, enculturated prejudices, it can also teach us to honor ourselves.

Though placing conditions upon those we love and those we allow to love us can be limiting, conditions can also serve us. When we set self-honoring standards (or conditions) for ourselves and for the people we choose to invite into our lives, we are living by our own personal principles.

As discerning, self-caring adults, we have the responsibility to develop conditions that honor us. For example, I am adamant about not allowing drug users or physical abusers into my personal life. I have established these conditions because they honor me.

As we continue to delineate and redefine our conditions, it is important to recognize the tenuous balance between principles we will realistically accept in a partner and prejudices created to sabotage a potentially intimate relationship.

We are all capable of attaining higher levels of love. Nevertheless, not having mastered those higher levels, we tend to "play it safe" and love conditionally. The fact is, most of us spend much of our time on the first three levels of love—Security Love, Sensuality Love, and Conditional Love. Undoubtedly, the level of Conditional Love is the most highly populated.

Level Four: Unconditional Love

The fourth level of any process is pivotal. This level can serve as the springboard to propel you forward to unknown heights, or it can keep you stuck and tangled in a quagmire. Unconditional Love is the fourth and pivotal level of love. Unconditional Love is the willingness and ability to love others only because they *are*. Unconditional Love is based solely upon the fact that the other person exists. Job, social status, or background are of no consequence. There are no conditions, no expectations, no hidden agendas—only love.

The Miracle of Unconditional Love

Although it is difficult to find a consistent model of Unconditional Love, the most steadfast love I have ever experienced in my life came from my friend Jason. Jason loved me unconditionally. No matter what my mood, appearance, or behavior, Jason loved me. His consistency made me want to give to him, loving him with the same quality he gave to me. His love made me want to stretch and grow.

Jason and I were inseparable for his entire life. Even on the night he died, Jason said good-bye to me and the world with loving eyes and a warm lick to my cheek. Jason was my best friend for many years. Some would say Jason was just a dog, but to me he was much more. He opened my heart and taught me about Unconditional Love. I can never forget that feeling or the times I have experienced that gift since.

Unconditional Love is special beyond words, and in that very specialness is the catch. It would be so gratifying to rejoice in the rare and colorful gem of Unconditional Love that we might never strive for more. We could be content to stay at this level and never move on, thus getting stuck in the quagmire I mentioned before. That is why this is the fourth and pivotal step of the levels of love. However, once we begin to discover the wonderful gifts of Unconditional Love, we can give ourselves permission to move ahead or to stay.

Personally, I believe if each and every one of us experienced this level of love at least once, our time here would be well spent. If we are willing to love just one person unconditionally, we can open the door for future generations to explore the higher levels of love.

The Higher Levels of Love

The last three levels of love—World Love, Universal Love, and Cosmic Love—are levels I have not yet experienced. But I have included them because they do exist. It is my guess that one day these higher levels of love will become the lessons for future generations. Albert Einstein beautifully summarized the synergistic feelings of all three of these higher levels of love:

> *A human being is a part of the whole, called by us "Universe," a part limited in time and space. He experiences himself, his thoughts and feelings as something separated from the rest—a kind of optical delusion of his consciousness. This delusion is a kind of prison for us, restricting us to our personal desires and to affection for a few persons nearest to us.*
>
> *Our task must be to free ourselves from this prison by widening our circle of compassion to embrace all living creatures and the whole of nature in its beauty.*

Lovingness

Loving yourself or someone else is a learned skill. Since there is so much to learn about the art of loving, let's explore a concrete way to practice loving by detailing The Seven Steps of Loving.*

Giving

The first component of loving is *giving.* Giving to ourselves is something our society frowns upon. We have been taught from a very early age to think of the other person first. Yet, as we have discussed repeatedly, if we do not give to ourselves first, we are soon empty vessels trying to fill another's cup. When we attempt to do the impossible—give when we have nothing left—we feel frustrated, embittered, and unappreciated. These are the seeds of martyrdom.

Giving to ourselves includes, but is not limited to, time

*Lazaris, *Loving*, © 1986 NPN Publishing, Inc.

to be alone, time to have fun, and time to share intimately with others. For example, when we spend the time it takes to grow and learn, we give to ourselves in a very tangible way. When we give to ourselves, giving in a romantic relationship becomes fun. Giving in a romantic relationship can range anywhere from little surprise gifts to giving the time it takes to communicate with meaning. Giving to ourselves or others is limited only by our imagination.

Responding

The next component of loving behavior is *responding*. Responding to the world around us in a way that honors us is also a learned skill. Too often, you and I react rather than respond. When we react impulsively, we do not serve ourselves or anyone else. Responding means we have taken the time to think and feel before we act. This may take a matter of moments or several days.

Responding to life is the crux of responsibility. Being responsible means we are both willing and able to respond to ourselves and others in ways that honor us. In romantic relationships, we can respond, or act responsibly, by taking care of our own needs before we respond to the relationship.

In my relationship with Jonathan, our behavior degenerated to the point of reaction rather than responding. Neither one of us wanted to be responsible for our own needs. We both wanted the other person to be the first to demonstrate love. Because we both refused to respond first to ourselves and then to each other, we were left with the wounded feelings reacting always causes. How could we be responsible for creating a loving relationship if we couldn't even respond to our own needs?

Respect

Respect is the next component of loving behavior. Self-respect is the ability to honor the depths of our emotions.

The intensity of our emotions is another part of us we have never been taught to appreciate. One of the many things we have been learning in this book is to recognize and experience the depths of our feelings by acknowledging them and exploring their meanings.

After we have been self-respecting by recognizing and experiencing our feelings, we can decide whether to respond to them. Self-respect encompasses acknowledging and experiencing the total range and spectrum of our emotions.

In a romantic relationship, respect means we are willing to acknowledge our partner's emotional nature. This includes our willingness to accept the fact that our partner's emotional nature may be totally different from our own. Respect means learning to honor our partner's feelings even when they are totally incongruous to our own.

Knowing

Knowing is yet another component of loving. Let's take a look at why knowing ourselves and our partner is an integral part of loving behavior.

Have you ever had the empty feeling of someone telling you how much she or he loves you, yet you know that person does not know the "real" you? For many of us, not being known is much more painful than not being loved. For how can someone profess love for us without investing the time or energy it takes to know us?

When someone we care about explores the intricacies we possess, this gift of loving behavior touches the deepest core of us. To be seen, to be heard, to be understood, to be known for all that we are—and are not—is one way we can experience love.

Taking the time to know and understand ourselves is a part of loving. In a romantic relationship, taking the time to know and understand our partner is loving behavior.

Humility

Humility is another component we must practice as we develop the skill of loving. Humility for most of us brings up images of bowed heads, apologetic glances, and groveling. However, *humility* is another of those words we need to reevaluate in new light.

Because most of us move automatically from day to day, basing our decisions, desires, and expectations on our past experiences, we limit our ability to love. Humility is our willingness to allow every day to be new.* This means we can experience every day without preconceived ideas about how it "should" be.

When we begin to develop this kind of humility, we can release ourselves and others from behavioral patterns that are based on the past. Humility means allowing newness in the here and now.

Humility is also an important component of romantic relationships. We enter romantic relationships with preconceived ideas about the opposite sex, opinions or prejudices about men and women that diminish us as human beings. We also develop similar opinions about our individual partners, especially about behavior we dislike. With humility as a component of our loving relationship, however, we can allow our partners to choose new patterns of behavior. For example, if your partner always wakes crabby, humility allows her or him the space to wake up and choose her or his own emotions, whatever they may be.

Humility allows us to forgive the past and to move beyond. My clients Paul and Jane saw a dramatic change in their relationship when they developed the skill of humility. Initially, they came to see me fearing their relationship was over. They thought there was "too much water under the bridge" to save

---

*Definition by Lazaris.

it. Neither believed they could forget, much less forgive, the past. Just as important, neither believed the relationship could change to be loving and supporting.

They were willing, however, to make one last effort. They agreed to examine their expectations of themselves, each other, and the relationship. Once they began to realize that many of their unhealthy expectations kept them locked in past behavior, harming them and their relationship, they could experience genuine humility. As they released these expectations, the relationship was given a breath of new life. Their willingness to see themselves and their relationship in a new light freed them from the past, allowing them to create a new future. Humility allows a relationship the room it needs to grow and flourish.

Courage to Commit

Another component of loving behavior is the *courage to commit*. Being loving to ourselves means having the courage to commit to whatever feelings, thoughts, and behaviors honor us. Getting this far in *When Fairy Tale Romances Break Real Hearts* has taken tremendous courage on your part. You have repeatedly been asked to notice and explore aspects of yourself that are not easy to examine. You have advanced to this chapter because you are courageous, but also because you are committed to your self-growth.

Much of our fear of commitment is preprogrammed from our culture. Too often, we think commitment means being locked in and constrained. As products of our society, we have not allowed commitment to be a growing, breathing, regenerating part of our relationships. Perhaps there is a more accurate way to perceive courage and commitment.

The word *commit* comes from Latin, meaning to send or bring together. The origin of the word *courage* is French, meaning heart or, more loosely, spirit. Therefore, the "courage to commit" is the heart energy needed in order to inspirit a coming together, or relationship, either with ourselves, another, or both.

In a romantic relationship, commitment means developing principles that are honoring, nurturing, and celebrative of the individuals involved. Commitment is our joyous and voluntary agreement to operate by these principles. Some examples of principles include monogamy, honesty, and communication.

In establishing relationship principles that both partners can honor, it is important to discuss individual principles at each crossroads of the relationship. Some crossroads might include becoming sexually intimate, traveling together, living together, having children, and getting married.

In the relationship my clients Lee and Ann created, commitment to mutually enlivening principles was more than just words. One of the basic principles Lee and Ann agreed to was honesty in all things, even when it might be uncomfortable. When Lee first came to see me, he sought therapy to help sort out some feelings he did not understand. When he asked Ann to give him some time to work out his feelings, he assured her he would share everything he learned with her.

Because of the relationship they had built, because of their commitment, Lee was able to honestly express his feelings of confusion and his need for time and space to work them out. Ann, on the other hand, did not feel frightened or intimidated by Lee's need to work out feelings without her immediate input. She knew he would openly communicate with her when he was able.

Lee and Ann's principle of honesty had a track record they both trusted. Their commitment allowed a potentially explosive situation to be confronted without undue stress on Lee, Ann, or the relationship.

Caring

The final component of loving is *caring*. Caring is a state of being rather than an action. Self-caring means developing an attitude of gentleness toward ourselves, having compassion and forgiveness for ourselves.

In romantic relationships, we must also learn to be gentle and compassionate with our partners and their feelings. In the previous example, Ann demonstrated care for Lee with her compassion for his disorientation and confusion. Lee was caring of himself by asking for what he needed—time and space to explore his feelings.

Balancing the skills of caring for ourselves and our partner are not nearly as difficult when we are caring for ourselves first.

You can learn to utilize all the components of loving by evaluating your current patterns. The following Homegrowth will help you ascertain how well you treat yourself on a daily basis.

Homegrowth 16: How Do I Love Me?

(1) In your journal, list the seven components of loving behavior, leaving space for three additional columns to the right of your list.

Giving
Responding
Respect
Knowing
Humility
Courage to Commit
Caring

(2) Once a day, reviewing each component, evaluate how loving you were to yourself. Write down what you noticed in the column to the right of the list of seven components.

EXAMPLE:

Giving: I woke up late, hurried to work, went immediately from work to a meeting, returning home late with just enough energy to fall into bed.

Responding: I refused an invitation to a family gathering. I don't enjoy my family, and consequently it would be more self-honoring not to go.

---

(3) In the next column over, give a numerical value on a scale of 1 to 10 for each of the seven components.

EXAMPLE:
Giving: 1
Responding: 10

---

(4) In the last column, keep an account of what you have noticed.

EXAMPLE:

Giving: When I am rushed and have myself scheduled hectically, I neglect myself.

Responding: It felt good to have my feelings come first.

---

(5) Continue this exercise for at least three weeks.

After a few weeks of evaluating, you will be monitoring your behavior automatically. This self-awareness will help you make decisions that are more loving.

Loving behavior is clearly a learned skill. Like all skills, at first we might feel clumsy and uncomfortable. As we practice and become more proficient, we can relax and allow the skill of loving to become a "natural" part of us. When we give, respond, respect, know, demonstrate humility, develop the courage to commit, and care, we are practicing the skill of love.

Like other processes, *When Fairy Tale Romances Break Real Hearts* has a pivotal level, and like other processes, it is the fourth level. In Chapter Four, we have taken a definitive step toward learning about the true nature of love. As we progressed through the various levels of love, we learned that we alone can offer ourselves security; we can enjoy but not survive on sensuality; and that placing conditions on others before we will love them can be self-limiting as well as self-honoring. We learned about the challenges of loving unconditionally and even took a peek at the loftier levels of love.

However, because this chapter is the fourth and pivotal level, it is up to us to choose once more. We may decide we now know all there is to know about loving relationships, close this book, and put it on the shelf. Or we may choose to pursue this thing called love by continuing to discover why it has eluded us for so long.

In my own process, I had without a doubt enjoyed exploring the various levels of love with Jonathan. But because I continued to feel sad and lonely, I chose to pursue that silent thief of love, loneliness.

Chapter Five
Know Thyself
(The Oracle of Apollo at Delphi)

Sometimes in the endless night, when I was without Jonathan, sleep refused to creep in and end my misery. I was so
consumed with loneliness I felt as if a hundred thousand mag-
gots were devouring my being. I played sad love songs and
cried while a pack of coyotes, roaming near my home, mocked
me with their lonesome howls. The wind rustled through
the trees, whispering words I never heard. I only knew no
one had ever suffered such loneliness.

The preceding scenario seems embarrassingly melodramatic now. Yet if we are impeccably honest, most of us can
probably recount similar experiences. At one time or another,
all of us have felt such overwhelming devastation evoked by
that overwhelming emotion we all have shared: loneliness.

Quite simply, I was lost in the melodrama of unrequited
love, and all I knew was loneliness; overriding loneliness engulfed everything I did. So, needless to say, my own loneliness became the focus, leading the way on my new search
toward self-understanding.

Loneliness

The Silent Thief

What is it about loneliness that seems to haunt so many of us? Everywhere we go, we can see it reflected in one another's eyes. Poets lament empty hearts, song writers dramatize lonely nights, and novelists expound upon the human condition—loneliness. I knew that somehow I needed to find an explanation to help me understand my pervasive feelings of loneliness.

I searched the professional literature for "loneliness," and found it was treated like the common cold; though the feeling was "controllable," the literature stated, it was also "inevitable." To me, these explanations were trite and superficial. Nothing I read could explain the momentous impact of loneliness.

I knew there had to be much more to this phenomenon called loneliness, so I continued my research. I questioned everyone I knew, from friends and colleagues to clients and family, about personal perspectives of loneliness.

Professionals and laypeople alike spoke of their experiences as if they were experts. They spoke of the lasting effects of loneliness and their own personal battles with it. All of them spoke of the lingering fear of having to combat the loneliness monster in the future. Because loneliness had been so devastating, the focus for most was to avoid loneliness at all cost.

If loneliness and the fear of it could allow us to lose innumerable nights of sleep, it was evident loneliness was potent enough to hold us captive in other, more self-destructive, behavioral patterns. For example, some of us attempt to protect ourselves from the pain of loneliness by working obsessively, shopping compulsively, or abusing food, drugs, and sex to diminish our feelings.

As I began putting more of the pieces of the loneliness puzzle together, a complex and perplexing picture began to emerge. I decided loneliness was incredibly dangerous because so many of us allow it to rob us of security, love, and personal power. Loneliness was nothing less than a thief, a silent thief that steals in the night. Because we fear being left all alone, we allow ourselves to be held hostage, the ransom being our confidence and personal power.

I continue to be amazed at how many of us are still willing to accept loneliness as a condition of love, like taxes or death. The physical ache of loneliness follows many of us everywhere. We feel alone when we are with other people, at work, at school, and even while we are making love. Unfortunately, our acceptance makes it all the more insidious.

The ache becomes so familiar we almost forget to notice it—almost. Some of us stop trying to fill the empty places within. We give up all hope the pain will ever leave. When we give up hope, a part of us is gone, stolen by this insidious thief—loneliness.

Perhaps it is time to shed some light on this obscure topic. Perhaps if we can define and understand loneliness, we can learn it need never rob us of ourselves again.

Seven Types of Loneliness

Loneliness seems so unfathomable partly because we believe it is a curse we must live with. However, loneliness itself is far more complex than we ever imagined. Only when I began to learn about the different types of loneliness, could I begin to understand its complexity.

There are many kinds of loneliness.* I have chosen the seven most common types to outline here.

Mourning

Mourning is the natural experience that occurs after any loss.

*Lazaris, *Ending Loneliness*, © 1986 NPN Publishing, Inc.

Nostalgia

Nostalgia is that bittersweet sorrow that we experience when we remember the past. Listening to old love songs, reading old love letters, or looking at picture albums can elicit the lonely feeling called nostalgia.

Lonely Future

The *Lonely Future* is not knowing what, if anything, is next in our lives. The fantasy of a future filled with nothing causes this kind of loneliness.

Abandonment

Abandonment embodies all our feelings of being deserted because we are not good enough. Some of us fear this type of loneliness so much we sacrifice our very personhood and greatly dishonor ourselves by staying in unhealthy relationships. Another level of this type of loneliness is self-abandonment—that is, we disconnect from ourselves. In a vain attempt to escape the pain within, some of us abandon all connection with ourselves and with our inner truths. Self-abandonment can create feelings such as "I'll never be good enough to love," which lead to our inability to create or maintain romantic relationships.

Being Alone

Being Alone is considered by some to be the ultimate loneliness. Some of us will do almost anything in order not to be alone.

Despair

Despair is a form of loneliness much rarer than we might believe. Despair is "hopelessness with the illusion of helplessness."* You and I might occasionally feel deep levels of

---

*Lazaris, *Ending Loneliness*, © 1986 NPN Publishing, Inc.

self-pity, but few of us have ever really tasted the acid pain of despair. Perhaps this is what many of our teenagers feel when they choose to end their own lives.

Beautiful Sadness

Beautiful Sadness is the final type of loneliness I will discuss here. If you wonder how sadness can be beautiful, think about walks on misty, rain-filled nights with a lonesome foghorn moaning in the distance.

When I was introduced to these different kinds of loneliness, I also discovered their power. Ultimately, loneliness has power over us because we have been taught to fear it. We use our fear, rather than the loneliness itself, to "keep ourselves in line."

Our parents used loneliness to mold and manipulate us. We all remember statements such as: "Stop crying or go to your room" . . . *and be alone.* "If you are not good, I'm going to leave you right here" . . . *and you will be alone.* "If you don't smile and be nice to the other children, no one will like you" . . . *and you will be alone.* The unspoken part of parental threats was often the implication we had to do it their way or suffer the damnation of being alone.

The fact is, when we were very young, being alone was life threatening. We knew this and feared the possibilities of what being alone would mean. Now that we are adults, however, many of us have failed to release our childhood fears. Consequently, we still believe being alone will ultimately destroy us—and we act accordingly.

As I allowed this information to seep in, I noticed things I had never seen before. For instance, when I walked through shopping malls, I would hear parents speaking to their children. Incredulously, I watched fear grow in the eyes of the children. More times than not, the threat these parents used to control their children was aloneness or abandonment. I actually saw parents take a few steps away from their children, using fear—the fear of loneliness—to control and manipulate their offspring.

If we look, we can find examples of this type of manipulation everywhere. Advertising firms use a similar type of manipulation in order to control our buying habits. If you don't brush your teeth with product X, no one will like your smile, no one will want to kiss you, and you will be alone. If you don't drive a certain type of car, if you don't use a certain brand of breath mint, if you don't live in a certain area of town, if you don't wear a certain type of clothing—all of these relate the same familiar message. Implicit or explicit, the message is always identical: "If you don't do the right thing, *you will be alone.*"

With this type of barrage attacking us from infancy on, it is not surprising that loneliness or the threat of it has become so devastating and so absolutely immobilizing.

When I took a close look at the pathetic, melodramatic behavior I described in the first paragraph of this chapter, I realized I had, indeed, allowed loneliness to immobilize me. The only way I could diminish this fear and release myself from its clutches was to accept the fact that the only power this loneliness monster had was the power I was willing to give it. Before I could do this, however, I needed to learn to recognize my feelings of loneliness and the immobilizing fear they imposed upon me.

I chose to use the process of journaling to learn about my feelings of loneliness because journaling is simple, and it is one of the most effective tools we have for enhancing self-awareness. The process of actually writing about our thoughts helps us take them out of the abstract and accept their reality. As we attempt to make sense of our feelings and thoughts by actually writing about them, we force ourselves to look more deeply within and thus gain a better insight into our behavior.

In order for a journal to be effective, we must strive to be absolutely honest in writing our thoughts and feelings. No one else need ever read your personal journal.

Homegrowth 17: Discovering Your Personal Loneliness

(1) In your journal, create a section for loneliness.

→ Use one page for each of the seven types of loneliness discussed above.

Mourning
Nostalgia
Lonely Future
Abandonment
Being Alone
Despair
Beautiful Sadness

(2) Using your past experiences, describe an incident for each type of loneliness you have personally experienced.

→ Be sure to describe how you *felt* at the time.

In order to illustrate this process more effectively, I want to share a page out of my own journal. It deals with the mourning aspect of loneliness.

When I was a freshman in college, my favorite uncle died. To describe him merely as "my favorite uncle" is to diminish his impact on my life. Uncle Howie was the only male who allowed me to feel safe and loved during the early part of my life. As I look back over the bleak harshness of my childhood, Uncle Howie provided an oasis of safety. But, more important, he was the one man in my young life who offered me joy, love, and safety. For my journal entry under "Mourning,"

I chose to write my remembrances of the day my Uncle Howie died.

21 December 1972

When my mom called this morning, there was panic in her voice. "Grandma just called and said Uncle Howie had another heart attack and is lying on the rug in the hall between the bedrooms. She wants you to come right over."

My reply was just as panicky. "I can't get there any faster than the paramedics. Hang up the phone and tell her to call the paramedics. I'm on my way."

I remember shaking as I put the key in the ignition of my car. I don't remember getting to my uncle's house; I just remember running in the door and standing where I knew his body had been. My mother arrived shortly thereafter and found me standing in the hallway staring at the empty carpet.

She grabbed me by the shoulders, turned me around, and said, "They went to the hospital."

I don't remember driving to the hospital either. Yet, suddenly I was there. In the waiting room outside intensive care, I remember standing next to one of those ashtrays that seem to exist only next to hospital elevators. I remember offhandedly thinking my uncle wasn't supposed to smoke any more—not since his first heart attack. I also remember thinking I knew he smoked secretly. I don't think I stood in that waiting room long, but again, I just don't remember.

My Aunt June came out of the ICU doors quietly. She had tears in her eyes when she looked at me and said, "Your Uncle Howie is gone."

I just looked at her. I wanted to ask if I could go in and see him. Somehow I wanted to make the fact he was dead untrue. I wanted to tell her she was lying, but

I didn't. I just stood there and stared at her, and at my mother and my grandmother, who were also waiting with me. How strange we must look, I thought, four women alone in the ICU waiting room. My mother, my grandmother, and now my Aunt June had all lost their husbands. I had lost a father, a grandfather, and, now, I had lost one of the most precious human beings in my young life. I had lost my Uncle Howie.

As I wrote these words in my journal and reexperienced those intense feelings of mourning, one thing became clear. I realized this type of loneliness is not life threatening. Mourning had not killed my aunt, my mother, my grandmother, or me. I was still alive, and I did not even *want* to die. I was just terribly, terribly sad.

Where was the terror that attaches itself to loneliness? What had happened to those threats of childhood, those manipulations of parents, advertising firms, and society? True, I was incredibly sad—I was experiencing loneliness—but contrary to what I had always been taught, I was just fine.

As I progressed in my journal through the various kinds of loneliness—Nostalgia, Lonely Future, Abandonment, Being Alone, Despair, and Beautiful Sadness—I continued to learn the same lesson. Each time I reexperienced another aspect of loneliness, I released the emotional burden of carrying it.

As I continued this process, I also freed myself of the feelings that loneliness might destroy me. The more loneliness I allowed myself to feel, the more I was able to release and the freer I became.

Little by little, I realized it was actually I who controlled the power of my loneliness. Once again, I learned that the responsibility, and the choice, was mine. Now that I understood loneliness and its power more clearly, I could choose to let it control my life or I could simply see it clearly for what it is: an emotion I sometimes experience.

Unless we allow it, loneliness—in and of itself—is not capable of crippling or immobilizing us. Loneliness, then, is nothing more than another feeling we experience. Most important, loneliness needs to be recognized and experienced—not feared.

As usual, merely *knowing* loneliness is simply a feeling was not enough for me. Now that I knew what loneliness was, I wanted to learn when and where I experienced it. Precisely when did feelings of loneliness begin to invade my being?

The Onset of Loneliness

Though many circumstances may cause feelings of loneliness, I learned it always occurs with a sudden shift in expectations. The operative words are *sudden shift.* That our expectations may be positive or negative has little or no impact on *when* we experience loneliness. Loneliness is a phenomenon of both the shift in expectations and the rapidity with which it occurs.

When I reviewed my "Fear of Loneliness Journal," I found that a sudden shift in my expectations precipitated each bout of loneliness. Most important, I noted the positive or negative aspect of my expectations had nothing to do with the feelings of loneliness that accompanied the sudden shift.

For example, at one point in my career, I was suddenly— without any prior anticipation—promoted to chief therapist. As I made my way home on the evening of my promotion, I realized that I was feeling sad and lonely instead of proud and elated as I might have expected. Then I realized that I had expected to maintain my current status. With the promotion, however, these expectations had suddenly shifted.

The type of loneliness I was experiencing at this time was Being Alone. I thought if I were promoted, I would be separated from my friends and co-workers—I would be alone. I was surprised to learn I could experience loneliness even when the sudden shift in expectations was ostensibly a positive one. Any sudden shift in expectations can move us into loneliness.

Beyond Loneliness

As I reviewed my new understanding of loneliness, I noticed a strange uneasiness beginning to irritate my awareness. Why had I created this loneliness in the first place? I wondered. (By this point, I knew I was responsible for creating all my feelings.) But now, my question was, *Why?* What purpose did creating loneliness serve?

Perhaps loneliness was merely camouflaging a stronger feeling. I began to wonder if there was something that frightened me even more than loneliness. My stomach contracted violently when that thought stomped its way through my body. After all, what could be more terrifying than loneliness?

I had worked long and hard learning about loneliness. Could there possibly be more to learn? If not, why was something continuing to fester in my gut?

I was sitting on my porch looking at the city lights twinkling in the valley below. They sparkled like earthbound stars. They seemed to reflect the night sky to me. I still remember the sadness I felt, wishing Jonathan was with me to share the magic of the night. If only Jonathan could just relax and let me love him. All he had to do was receive the love I had to give.

As I continued my musing, my eyes wandered to the stars again, then to the city lights, then back to the stars. Suddenly, a black fog seemed to cloud my vision. In that moment, I realized that just as the lights and the stars appeared to reflect one another, so did Jonathan and I.

After all the time I had spent blaming Jonathan for not letting me love him, now I recognized I was doing the very same thing—I was not allowing him to love me. I had not noticed that we were both refusing to be loved because we acted out our fear of receiving love in different ways. He manifested his fears of receiving love by creating long separations. I manifested similar fears by creating a connection with a man who could only give of himself sporadically.

This revelation was so phenomenal I lost track of time and space. It was only the bite of the cold mountain air that brought me back to physical awareness. As I moved indoors to the warmth of the fireplace, I also moved back into old memories, memories that began to illuminate the truth: It was not only Jonathan; I, too, was afraid of receiving love.

As I reviewed my past relationships with other men, a pattern began to emerge. In general, the men in my life had loved me, yet I had not experienced their love. They had cherished and praised my ability to love, yet unknowingly, I held myself distant from their love. Clearly, my unwillingness to receive love was one more issue only I could resolve.

To Receive or Not to Receive— That Is the Question

Who would knowingly throw love away? We all have at one time or another. We have rejected prospective lovers because they did not suit us. We have turned down proposals of love, marriage, and friendship for a wide range of rationalized reasons. (Remember Homegrowth 15, What Condition Are Your Conditions in?) However, the truth is, many times we are simply running from love, afraid to risk what receiving love might feel like.

When I learned I had foolishly thrown love away, I was amazed. With this discovery, I began another search, this time for the reasons I was prohibiting myself from receiving love.

Like so many of my other self-imposed limitations, this one was also based on fear, and once more, fear left over from my past. Since I had not recognized this fear, I could not resolve it. By this time, I knew if I could discover *why* I was afraid to receive love, I would create the opportunity to resolve my fear of being loved. I would be able to stop bringing my past into my present.

In order to do this, however, I had to be willing to explore some of the horrible memories from my past and learn how these were still affecting my present and my future. I knew both my conscious and subconscious memories would continue to influence me until I acknowledged and understood them.

I began my search for understanding my past with conscious memories that were readily available to me. The following is a description of the conscious remembrance that began my journey toward learning why I was afraid to receive love.

My eyes snapped open as the first piercing scream crashed through the walls of our house. I didn't have to think; I knew. My mother's sobs were clearly audible as they floated up the heating duct to the bedroom on the second floor. I was frozen inside, afraid to move and afraid not to.

"Stop, please stop!" The cries of my mother drove me to my feet. Another scream sent my sister into wild sobs as we now stood in the middle of our room, children in long flannel pajamas, shivering not from the winter cold but from the terror we were hearing. Mindlessly, we started creeping down the darkened hall, pausing a moment at the top of the stairs. We could hear only muffled words now, so we descended farther into the terror below.

We found our parents in the front hall. My mother was curled into a ball, trying to protect herself from the pummeling of my father's fists. My father, his back to us, was hunched over in his cruel attempt to find a vulnerable spot to hit. Ludicrously, I noticed how bizarre he looked, naked except for his undershorts.

Though we said nothing, he sensed our presence and turned around, redirecting his bellowing rage toward us. Like panicked, pathetic deer, running from the senseless slaughter of a "sports" hunter, we ran screaming through the house as our out-of-control, drunken father followed in our wake.

I'm not sure how we made it back upstairs, but my sister's muffled cries under the covers brought me out of shock. I wanted to go to her and tell her we were okay, but I couldn't. I couldn't get my legs to move.

My mother appeared out of the darkened hallway and tried to comfort my sister. "Shhh, it's okay now; he's done."

"*He's done!*" Those words sent anger ripping through me. "He's done." As if he had been calmly eating dinner! I wanted to be comforted, too, but I also wanted my mother to *do* something. I wanted him locked up. I wanted him dead, gone— never, ever to return. I wanted him to hurt the way he had hurt my mother. I wanted to scream with terror and pain.

"Call the police," I said.

"I can't," my mother sighed. "I can't. They would lock him up. I can't do that. I love him."

She loved him? This was love? I simply could not understand my mother. And, if my father loved my mother, as he invariably said he did after each of his rages, then I wanted no part of it. I wanted no part of love. From my perspective, my first conscious memory about love was to decide it was safer *not* to love—or to be loved.

Perhaps your childhood was like mine, perhaps not. The scenario each of us experienced is different. Nevertheless, the results of childhood for far too many of us are the same. Somewhere long ago, probably before you were even five years old, you, too, might have made a similar decision that being loved was too frightening, too painful.

Contrary to what we were told, many of us observed that love meant being abandoned, hurt, manipulated, or abused. Consequently, we decided love was simply too risky.

From Birth or Perhaps Before

Children see, feel, and remember much more than we give them credit for. If you question the feasibility of a young child deciding love is too painful, remember that young children do not make these decisions on a conscious level. The child feels the pain. When pain seems to be in direct relationship to love, it does not take a child very long to associate the two.

We grow up recreating the same kind of "love" relationships we had as models—those filled with pain—until we finally learn love is to be avoided at all costs.

What if at two or three years of age, or perhaps earlier, you made a subconscious decision that being loved was unsafe? What if your entire life was based upon that decision, and what if that decision remained subconscious—that is, you failed to notice you had even made that decision?

Obviously, I had failed to notice I had made such a decision in my childhood. As a result, I had refused love all my adult life. The fact is, I had failed to notice I was refusing to be loved.

As we have already discussed, relationships have a way of allowing us to make new discoveries about ourselves. Although my relationship with Jonathan had allowed me to notice many things about myself, the fact that I had repeatedly failed to receive love was one of the most life-changing realizations I came to.

Immediate Response Technique

Before long, I began to wonder about others—my friends, my clients, my colleagues. Had they, too, made similar decisions about receiving love? Or was my childhood so out of the ordinary that I, alone, was affected?

Using a therapeutic technique I call Immediate Response, I began to explore the issue of receiving love with clients who came to me with relationship problems. This technique requires a spontaneous response to a properly phrased question.

With this technique, we are able to tap into parts of the subconscious with little or no difficulty. Allowing spontaneous insights into our childhood beliefs, decisions, and choices, the Immediate Response Technique does not explore conscious recall. Instead, it deals with the subconscious mind's knowledge of our past. My clients particularly enjoy this technique because of the instantaneous results.

Cindy first came to see me because her past relationships had not worked, and she wanted to give her current relationship a better chance.

It was apparent that the other aspects of Cindy's life worked. She was financially successful, attractive, and pleasant. Cindy's history with romantic relationships led us to explore her hidden fear of receiving love. In a very short period of time, we discovered that Cindy was terrified of being loved. She believed that being loved was synonymous with being hurt, and it was quite evident that her behavior honored her belief. What still puzzled her, however, was why she had formed that belief in the first place.

Using the Immediate Response Technique, we began to put the pieces of Cindy's past together. Sitting in the safety of my office, we began to work.

"Cindy, I want you to relax as much as you can, and simply answer my questions with the very first response that comes to your mind," I said. "If the response is delayed, I will simply ask the question in another way, so don't worry about it. Are you ready?"

"Yes."

"Okay, let's begin," I continued. "If you were to know how old you were when you decided love hurt, it would probably be at the age of _____ ?"

Cindy's response jumped from her mouth almost before the question was completed. "Three."

"If you were to know who you were with on that day you would know you were with _____ ?"

"Myself. I was alone. I'm alone and I don't understand why." Cindy began to cry. The technique had taken her back to an experience she had completely forgotten.

"Where are you, Cindy?"

"My room. I'm in my room sitting on the corner of my bed."

"If you were to know how you felt, you would know you felt
_____ ?" I asked.

"Sad," she said.

"If you were to know what happened to make you sad, what
probably happened was _____ ?"

"I was with my dad. He was watching the new babies."

Cindy and I continued our work and discovered that until
the age of three, she had been a pampered and petted only
child. Then her parents had twins and became very preoc-
cupied with the care of the new babies.

Later, as an adult, Cindy rationalized that her parents necessarily had to spend time with the twins. However, this ra-
tionalization had led her to deny the hurt feelings she had
experienced in childhood. As a child, she had perceived that
her parents had abandoned her in favor of her younger siblings.

Until we used the Immediate Response Technique, Cindy
was not aware of her feelings of abandonment or how they
had originated. Soon, Cindy began to realize that her pattern-
ing with men duplicated the feelings of her childhood. She
expected to be abandoned after a period of bliss. She successfully sabotaged each new loving relationship.

It didn't take Cindy long to discover that she had held onto her
childhood belief that love meant being abandoned. When she
realized this, she took the first step toward changing her belief.
(*Remember:* The first step in change is to *Notice* what we want
to change.) She learned exactly what her belief was and stated
it as concisely as possible: "Love means being abandoned."

When Cindy recognized she wanted to change this belief,
which no longer served her, she began to explore why she
created the belief in the first place. Cindy completed the first
phase of the second step of UnlimitedGrowth by writing her
answers to the Payoff Questions listed in Homegrowth 8,
Exploring the Why, in Chapter Three.

Remember: The second step in change is to *Acknowledge* by

a. *understanding* your behavior and how it serves you and
b. accepting responsibility for the *impact* of your behavior on yourself and others.

However, because Cindy did not fully comprehend the impact her behavior had on herself and the others in her life, she could not complete the second phase of Step Two. Cindy and I continued to explore the impact of her behavior until she could clearly see it. She noticed she pushed the men in her life away, creating circumstances that forced them to leave the relationship. Even when they tried to point out her behavior, she refused to see that it was she who was ending the relationships.

Cindy noticed that her anxiety level began to increase with the onset of every relationship. Every day was filled with the question "When will he abandon me?" To end the excruciating pain of anxiety, she actually facilitated the abandonment. Her fear of abandonment caused her daily anxiety and caused the men in her life the pain of helplessness and betrayal.

At this point, Cindy moved on to the third step in Unlimited-Growth, forgiving herself for what she had believed and consequently created. (*Remember:* The third step is to *Forgive.*)

Reaching Into the Depths

As more of my clients began to work through their pasts, I was busy working through my own. I, too, wanted to delve more deeply into the depths of my life. I knew that somewhere in my past I had formed beliefs I continued to act upon, yet I wasn't sure how or when these beliefs were formed.

I wanted to know why it was so important for me to "go it alone." In my life, I have often refused to ask for help, even when I desperately needed it. I truly wanted to know the answers to these questions, and I was willing to do whatever it took to get them.

Since I knew that these parts of my life were securely catalogued and stored in my subconscious, I needed to find a way to access the storage area. I was ready to learn new techniques to help me access my subconscious memories that were hidden and more difficult to reach.

This time, I turned to a technique called rebirthing,* a gentle and simple breathing technique that allowed me to break through my body's defense mechanisms. It permitted access into a realm of my life I had heretofore denied myself.

One of the life experiences recalled emotionally and physically by many who have used this technique is their own birth experience, hence the name "rebirthing."

In our society, feelings are not often acceptable, so we "swallow" them. In our effort to hold them down, our body stores this emotional energy. The function of the rebirthing process is to allow these pockets of emotional energy to be released. The releasing of this energy often brings up memories and emotions not easily accessible until this time. As the breathing process, or rebirthing, proceeds, energy continues to be released. Sometimes that release is demonstrated by spontaneous body movements and sounds.

Rebirthing is not a thinking process, but rather a process of allowing. Once I surrendered to the process, I allowed my body to move in whatever fashion it desired, and to make spontaneous sounds.

---

*It has been many years since I first experienced the rebirthing process I described here. Since then, the advances in the field of body memory have been significant. In my opinion, the most current and effective form of body memory work is *Bodydynamics*, taught by the Danish therapist Lisbeth Marcker. Her workshops and trained therapists are available in many areas. Those interested in learning more about rebirthing can find books and therapists in any metropolitan area in the United States.

At my first rebirthing workshop, I was able to regress to my actual birth experience. This is how I recalled this most extraordinary experience.

Once More—With Feeling

We had each been assigned a partner—a rebirther—to stay with us and facilitate the process by encouraging the breathing pattern. Our rebirthers breathed in the prescribed manner, allowing us to hear it and continue our own breathing in a similar pattern.

Lying in the safety of my private room, with my rebirther seated beside me, I had been doing the breathing exercise for what seemed like forever. I was frustrated because nothing seemed to be happening. As I listened to the steady breathing of my rebirther, the sound of his breathing encouraged me to mimic him. But it was hard to simply lie there and breathe; my mind jumped sporadically from one topic to another. Just as I was about to give up, my rebirther changed the breathing pattern, and I continued to try. One part of me seemed to be observing what was happening, while another part experienced it.

Finally, something inside me moved, and my body seemed to develop a will independent of my thought processes. I was amazed. My body wanted to move in a way I hadn't ordered and I allowed it to. As I followed my body's lead, my mind began to experience sounds, colors, and pictures.

I found myself stuck in a tight tube. It was dark and wet, and I was afraid. I tried to get out, but I couldn't move out of the darkness. I tried rotating my body and thumping my head against the walls that bound me. I tried kicking but found my feet had nothing to push against. I tried. I mean I really tried. All my energy was focused on getting unstuck.

The sweat rolled down the side of my body. I could taste the salt of my tears and feel the dampness of them in my ears. I had to get out. I started to panic. The tunnel continued to act as a living vise. I felt helpless. I wanted to scream, but I didn't.

Some internal part of me got mad—red, raging, I'll-do-it-myself mad! Instinctively, I knew someone was supposed to be doing this with me. I was furious because whoever was supposed to help had let me get stuck.

By this time, I realized I was reliving my birth experience. I tried not to think or rationalize but to allow the process to continue. I remember lying completely still and gathering energy; I let the rage fill me. I felt the stubbornness characteristic of my personality actually being born. Thoughts sprang into my mind: "If you won't help me, I'll do it alone. . . . Please help me."

Thoughts floated in and out, confusing and complicating. As I lay there stuck, fuming with rage, I was making intricate, life-molding decisions. The thoughts I experienced during the rebirthing I knew word for word—thoughts like, "If no one will help, I'll do it alone." "I don't need anyone, I can do this." "I'm so mad, I can do anything."

Finally, gathering all of my energy, I decided I would get out. How dare they leave me stuck and not help? I'd show them! So I twisted, turned, and pushed. Slowly, very slowly, I began to turn. As I turned, I slowly moved out into the blinding light. When I was finally free, I screamed and screamed and screamed.

Slowly, I came back to myself. The bed was a shambles. In my effort to get out of my imaged birth canal, I had not only replayed the scene in my mind, but also with my body.

Several minutes later, when I had enough energy, I recorded my experience on tape so I would not forget. I was far too weak to write, so I simply turned the tape recorder on and talked. As I talked out my thoughts and feelings, I could see how the foundations for my beliefs had been laid.

If you feel this was simply a fantasy created by hyperventilation and an overactive imagination, I assure you it was much more. Shortly after my rebirthing experience, I called my mother, who lives two thousand miles away, and described my experience. She was startled and awed because I knew things she had long forgotten. I shared feelings of fear and impatience with her, and I shared my urgent need to get out.

She, in turn, shared the incident that led to my birth—a traumatizing fight with my father. She went into labor prematurely. Until we discussed my rebirthing experience, I had never known that I was born one month premature. My parents' fight explained not only the fear I had experienced, but also my overpowering drive to get out.

As we discussed more of my feelings, my mother explained hers. During labor, she was exhausted emotionally and physically. She felt abandoned, discouraged, used, hurt, and resentful. All of which explains my feelings of abandonment. She simply had no energy left to help me get out of the birth canal. She remembers, however, that I came out of the womb red, mad, and screaming.

After our conversation, I was convinced I had achieved more than I had anticipated. Rebirthing allowed me to reexperience my personality traits being formed. I actually caught a glimpse of the interconnection of my beliefs and these personality traits. These traits included:

1. doing it alone, which accounts for my superindependence;
2. struggling and achieving;
3. being stubborn and tenacious, qualities that have both served and harmed me;
4. asking for help, yet not expecting it will come;
5. using anger as a motivating force.

I am still amazed that all of these traits were developed at birth. What appalls me more is how I have subconsciously accepted their existence without questioning whether they honored me.

It is important that we evaluate whether or not our personality traits currently honor who we want to be. We can begin this evaluation by discovering our personality traits.

Homegrowth 18: Getting to Know You

(1) Make an honest list of your personality traits.

(2) Ask those who know you (family, friends, lovers) to list your personality traits.

→ Get a list from as many people as possible.

(3) Compare the lists.

→ Do you feel the people in your life have an accurate picture of you?

→ Were you surprised at their insight or lack of insight?

(4) Compile a composite of all the lists to form an honest combination of your traits. On a separate sheet of paper with two columns, write your new list in the far left-hand column under the heading "Personality Traits."

(5) On the right-hand side of the paper, list the beliefs that may have led to the development of each specific trait.

EXAMPLE:

Personality Traits	*Beliefs*
Overcautious	The world is an unsafe place. I cannot trust anyone
Excessively independent	I cannot trust anyone. I can do it better than anyone.
Being a "good girl"	Love is earned. No matter how hard I try, he'll never love me.

(6) Notice any personality traits you would like to change.

→ Use the steps in UnlimitedGrowth outlined in Chapter Two to change.

Identifying and evaluating our personality traits is another pathway into ourselves. The more we discover about ourselves, the more consciously we can re-create ourselves.

In this chapter, we took another step toward reclaiming our personal power. We learned that loneliness is a feeling to be experienced and released. It is only our fear that made loneliness into a monster.

We learned about the tools of journaling, the Immediate Response Technique, and rebirthing. These tools can help us access our conscious as well as our subconscious memories, giving us greater insight into ourselves, our personality traits, and our beliefs.

Getting to know ourselves allows us to enter into deeper, more honest, and intimate relationships. Without this self-knowledge, we can never hope to know what true intimacy is all about.

Chapter Six
Intimacy

A few years ago, when I initially wrote this section, it was incredibly easy. However, as I reread this chapter, preparing it for final editing, I was appalled. Where was the depth, power, and beauty I had hoped to relate? Clearly, I had omitted *intimacy* from the very chapter that required it most!

At that moment, I realized that intimacy is the basic foundation of this book, and here I was trying to describe that most personal of human phenomena in objective, cognitive terms. When I reread all of my tidy definitions and didactic exercises, I realized I had failed to convey the essence of true intimacy. How do I write a teardrop? What words do I use to describe this depth of emotion we all yearn so dearly to experience? Where were the words I needed?

I thought back to the chapters I had already completed. I remembered writing about my parents' quarrels and about my Uncle Howie's death. I remembered the intensity of emotion it took to write about my rebirthing experience. Certainly I had already created a high level of intimacy in this book. Why then was writing about the specifics of intimacy so elusive?

I thought about this for a very long time. I took the time

to reexperience exactly what allowed me to create those instances of true intimacy between myself and my reader. I knew by exploring my feelings, I could find the clues I needed to build the kind of intimacy I wanted to experience when I reread this chapter for the last time. I was not disappointed.

Reviewing the processes I used in relating those intimate events in my life led to a major discovery about intimacy: Intimacy is a synergistic system.

Intimacy is a complete entity comprised of various components. Each component or skill necessary to create intimacy works toward accomplishing a purpose of its own. At the same time, however, all these skills work together to create a whole new concept that is in the shared interest of all. That new concept is intimacy. Briefly, the skills of intimacy are individually worthy and singularly important, yet, together, they create an unfathomable human experience.

Still, I was at a loss for words. How could I describe all that intimacy encompasses? The truth is, I cannot. Intimacy is, indeed, unfathomable because no one has ever experienced it in its entirety. It is a phenomenon similar to that of the atom. Though physicists have never actually seen an atom, they know it exists. They can describe how it works and even what it is composed of, yet no one has ever *seen* an atom.

So it is with intimacy. We see the effects of intimacy, but, like so much of our reality, we are not able to comprehend its enormity.

Intimacy is also infinite. No matter what level of intensity we create, there is always more. Intimacy, like our own self-exploration, is an ongoing, never-ending process.

Knowing all this, I continued to struggle, searching for a way to convey all I had learned about intimacy in a way that would honor its significance in human relationships. Finally, I remembered a lesson from a very dear friend and colleague, Michael Benner.

"Whenever or wherever you're lost or confused," he teaches,

"remind yourself to close your eyes, take a couple of slow, deep breaths, relax, and feel your mind opening, your awareness expanding, and watch and listen to the enhanced flow of good ideas, solutions, answers, goals, and desired outcomes. By choosing to feel safe, responsible, and relaxed, [we can] access maximum creativity."

And so it was that I remembered the blue sapphire.

Color Intimacy Blue

Since ancient times, the blue sapphire has been associated with intimacy. Long ago, wise old scholars postulated that the luminous blue of the sapphire vibrated at an intensity that nurtured intimacy.

Today, as psychologists continue to learn more about the role of color in our daily lives, it is apparent that different colors do affect us in various ways. Specifically, researchers have discovered that deep blue, commonly associated with the sapphire, can have the effect of creating feelings of calmness and safety which can ultimately foster an environment more conducive to intimacy.

Therefore, ancient wisdom, combined with modern technology, gave me the appropriate metaphor: Intimacy is like a radiant blue sapphire.

In order to fully comprehend this gem of intimacy, let's consider it first as a whole—a creation of spectacular beauty. However, before any facets can be cut into a gemstone, the stone itself must have integrity in the truest sense of the word. It must be whole and complete. This wholeness, this one binding force of intimacy is called *willingness*.

Where There's a Will, There's a Way

How many times have you heard that saying? Yet, did you ever feel certain things could not be accomplished no matter how hard you tried? Maybe you even *felt* like you gave up; maybe you even *thought* you stopped trying. Then perhaps when you expected it least, you finally created what you initially wanted.

The truth is, somewhere in the depths of yourself, you did not give up; you retained your willingness. Somewhere, a part of you continued to try without actively working at it.

As I have learned to consciously create my own reality, I have also learned about willingness. Willingness is magical, because it is the one thing that can open doors we thought were locked. It allows us to create what we want even when we think we have stopped trying. Willingness keeps us from giving up until we can create the reality we desire.

Conversely, our lack of willingness can affect our attitudes to the point of closing down any opportunity to create the reality we say we want.

Willingness is the one factor, the one common denominator, imperative to the function of each individual facet of intimacy. Without it, we would not allow ourselves to learn the skills necessary to create intimacy. Without willingness, we would not expend the time and energy to learn about intimacy; we would not be able to create even one of the facets.

The Facets of Intimacy

An Overview of the Gem of Intimacy

Since intimacy is such an intricate and detailed phenomenon, I have included a short synopsis of each of its seven facets before we consider them in depth. Inherent in each brief definition is the binding force of willingness.

> **Communication:** Sharing our thoughts and feelings authentically; honestly hearing and acknowledging what is being communicated to us.
> *Openness:* Sharing parts of us that are normally hidden away; a major component of communication.

Vulnerability: Exposing the tender-most parts of ourselves to the extent of possible hurt.

Nurturing: Caring and tenderness in our attitudes, behaviors, thoughts, and feelings, both toward ourselves and others.

Trust: Belief and confidence in ourselves and others.

Loving: Sharing and creating feelings of pleasure and safety with ourselves and others.

Knowing: Exploring the very core of our essence as well as that of others.

Courage: Moving beyond our own fears in our ongoing quest for self-truth.

These facets or components of intimacy are simply skills, skills we can learn and utilize. Each skill is designed, shaped, and polished to complement the others like the facets of a gem. As we become more adept at these skills, our proficiency in creating higher levels of intimacy will increase.

Communication

The language of friendship is not words but meanings.

Thoreau

The basis for any relationship, with ourselves or with others, is communication. The kind of communication needed for intimacy is not so much the stringing together of words. Rather, it is stringing thoughts and feelings together in a manner that conveys meaning both to ourselves and others. This is the language of friendship of which Thoreau spoke, and, for us, it will become the language of intimacy.

How do we learn to communicate our thoughts and feelings? Like many other first steps we have taken, we simply have to notice. Observing or noticing our behavior can teach us about our thoughts and feelings at any given moment. It becomes easier to communicate our thoughts and feelings once we know exactly what they are.

This skill teaches us to communicate within our own bodies, minds, and spirits. For example, recent research has demonstrated the advantages of communication between the mental and physical aspects of ourselves. Right and left brain research tells us communication between the two hemispheres allows us to integrate their various kinds of knowledge.

This kind of communication within ourselves gives us a better knowledge of who we are and what we really want to create in our lives. Open communication with ourselves can also foster open communication with others. When we know what we honestly think, feel, believe, and care about, we can communicate those aspects of ourselves to others. For if we do not know these things about ourselves, what is there to talk about but the weather?

In a romantic relationship, communication is even more imperative. We all yearn to share our true selves with another. Because we want someone to know us unadorned by any cosmetic or facade, we long to expose all the little secrets about ourselves, good and bad. We yearn to be touched and probed, and, after all that, we yearn for that other person to love us all the more.

However, if we lack self-communication skills, how can we possibly convey to another who we truly are? Before we can communicate our true essence, we must first know what the essence is.

Communicating or sharing the innermost depths—the very essence—of ourselves is called *openness*. Without openness, honest communication with ourselves, or in a romantic relationship, is an impossibility.

This type of openness does not include "true confessions." Confessions are made in order to receive absolution. Being open with another means we accept ourselves as we are. We suspend judgment and dispense with labels such as bad and good, accepting and embracing the marvelous complexity of ourselves.

When we choose to communicate openly in a romantic relationship, we want the person we love to experience the true essence of the self we have come not only to know and accept, but also to love and honor.

When I first learned about these facets of intimacy, this was one skill I *knew* I had mastered. After all, communication is my business—my life. Didn't I know all I had to know in order to communicate effectively and affectively with another?

I have often thought humility comes only after we have accumulated an abundance of knowledge, for it is then that we learn how little we actually know.

When I evaluated our communication skills, Jonathan and I got A's. I believed we were incredibly sophisticated at communicating with each other. After all, I used all the communications skills I knew at that time, focusing all my time and energy on exploring Jonathan's inner self. At that time, I never dreamed I had duped myself into believing Jonathan and I could talk about anything. Ah, how cunning I have been! And how humble I have become.

Because we worked so diligently on Jonathan's past, on his fears and dreams, I never paid much attention to the fact that Jonathan never knew *my* secret fears and dreams. Nor did I acknowledge my reluctance to *communicate* them to him.

He never even guessed about my fear he would leave me—or my fear he would stay. He never knew my dreams of being totally loved by him, and he never, never knew the pretty picture I had painted for our future together. I spent hours perfecting that picture, fantasizing how we would live together, creating a happy, loving home with mutually supportive careers.

Those were the dreams and fears I protectively tucked away,

never sharing them with Jonathan, never sharing them with anyone—until now. This, my friends, is not openness.

All Jonathan really knew about me was the warm, caring woman who was willing to walk the path of his life. I was that woman, but I was and am so much more.

Why didn't I share those secret fears and dreams with Jonathan? I thought of them as negatives, liabilities that needed to be covered up. I did not know their value. But my fears and dreams, no matter how I labeled them, were a part of the wonder and essence of me. Yet, I never dreamed that sharing those secret parts of me openly could endear me to anyone, especially Jonathan.

In other words, I thought that if Jonathan knew the real Kimberley Heart, he would not approve of her. I simply could not risk being vulnerable to the one man I truly loved.

Vulnerability

Vulnerability is the skill of exposing the most tender part of ourselves to be known and loved. When we communicate openly, we necessarily expose the more fragile elements of ourselves, and share these gifts with one another. It is one of the most unique and supreme acts of our humanness. If I had exposed my secret fears and dreams to Jonathan, I would have given both of us the gift of my vulnerability—a priceless commodity in the world of intimacy.

At the same time, the word *vulnerability* alone conjures up all sorts of ghosts and goblins. Too often, we believe if we are vulnerable, we will be hurt. Many of us simply do not want to take that risk, just as I did not want to risk communicating openly with Jonathan. Nevertheless, vulnerability does involve risk. When we are vulnerable, we risk being defenseless enough to be wounded or hurt.

Yet, unless we are willing to take that risk, we can never fully experience the essence of an intimate relationship with ourselves or anyone else. For vulnerability is at the very core of our humanness.

When I took a more honest look at my reluctance to communicate my secret fears and dreams with Jonathan, I realized I was too frightened to risk my vulnerability. I only knew that *vulnerable* was synonymous with *unsafe,* a word that meant I would undoubtedly be hurt.

Paradoxically, while I yearned for Jonathan to know the very depths of me, these were the very parts I worked relentlessly to conceal, to protect—even from myself. Interestingly, it was Jonathan who unwittingly helped me learn that *vulnerability* is not synonymous with *hurt.*

As I have said before, for me, Jonathan was a paragon among men. In my estimation, he was everything a prince worthy of Princess Kimberley should be. Yet, all those outward things— his looks, clothes, car, home, his finesse and popularity with people, men and women alike—never endeared him to me as much as the secret he was vulnerable enough to communicate openly to me, the secret he had never shared with anyone else.

I am sure all of you can remember similar incidents. For these are the times that warm our hearts and endear those we love to us; these are the magic times—the times we say to ourselves, "My God, I do love this person." I remember this particular incident clearly, and I will remember it just as clearly for all time.

Jonathan had driven up to the mountains to spend the weekend with me. Together, we dressed and roasted a small turkey with all the trimmings, sharing the meal with our dogs, Jason and Fargo. A magical bonding can take place simply by sharing a meal, a closeness the environment alone can foster.

After dinner, we sat side by side on the sofa in front of the blazing fire, the dogs snoring gently on the rag rug at our feet. "Isn't it amazing?" Jonathan mused. "We talk all the time and there's still so much to talk about."

I certainly understood what he meant, but I also knew the

importance of silence in communication. For a very long while, we simply watched the fire in silence.

"Believe it or not," Jonathan spoke again, "there are a lot of things you still don't know about me, a lot of things I never told you . . . but there is one thing I have been wanting to tell you for a long time."

My look acknowledged I had heard and understood. Again Jonathan was quiet for a long time before he continued. "I have never told anyone this, Kimberley. But for some reason, I want to tell you, I *need* to tell you."

He went on to explain how many years before, when he was a very young boy, he had been sexually abused. He had remembered only after many years. At first he told himself that it was just a fantasy, but when the images and feelings would not abate, he began to tell himself the truth. Clearly, the devastation was still with him. He ran away from this part of his life rather than look at it more closely. Therefore, it became more and more of a monster to him.

In that moment, Jonathan revealed to me what he had been afraid to share with anyone else, a secret he had barely come to integrate into himself. In sharing this most intimate painful story of his past, Jonathan had explored new depths of his vulnerability.

I learned a lot about vulnerability from Jonathan. The fact was, he was willing to risk what I could not. He openly shared his secret fears and dreams—even the ones he thought were negative. Instead of rejecting him, or finding him not enough, those secrets only endeared him to me more. His willingness to be vulnerable fostered a deeper connection with himself and with me. I will always cherish Jonathan's willingness to trust me with his vulnerability.

I sometimes wonder if I had been willing to take the same risk with him, if I had allowed him to see the true essence of me—all my scars and wounds—would I have been more endearing to him?

As I continued delving deeper into my own vulnerability, I began to understand the significance of nurturing as a facet of intimacy. Nurturing myself—treating myself with gentleness and kindness—nurtured my ability to be vulnerable. It also allowed me to be nurturing to Jonathan.

Nurturing

When we are tender and caring with ourselves and others, we are practicing the skill of nurturing. For instance, whenever Jonathan became vulnerable with me, as in the example just given, my warmth, understanding, and tenderness were nurturing to him.

Nurturing is not mothering or parenting. Rather, it is tenderness in both word and action. This skill offers both emotional and spiritual support.

Nurturing works in a very interesting way. Our willingness to be vulnerable allows us to be nurtured; yet, nurturing can foster vulnerability.

The night Jonathan shared his secret with me, he also revealed his pain. I understood that. I held him and listened as he disclosed the story he had kept hidden for so long. At that moment, I loved him for his humanness, his vulnerability.

After his tale was told and his tears were spent, the real nurturing began. There are many words I could have spoken at this time. But I didn't need to. I was nurturing to Jonathan by simply listening and stroking his head or back. By restating parts of his story when I might have misunderstood, and by asking questions such as, "You felt hurt [sad, mad, lonely]?" which helped clarify his feelings, he felt heard and understood.

I made no judgments, for true nurturing holds no place for judgments. Jonathan's humanness reached out and touched my own. He could not have received the warm nurturing I extended if he had not been so vulnerable. And I could never have given without judging, without rancor, if it were not for my own vulnerability.

For that brief shining moment in time and space, I saw the true essence of Jonathan, and he was also able to glimpse mine. The connection we felt is the *magic*—what life is all about. Not only did we connect in the manner human beings were originally meant to, we were at one with the All That Is. At a sacred and spiritual level, we experienced the humility, the awe, and the enormous responsibility involved in this wonder of being human.

Nurturing myself has become a very important aspect of my personal and professional life. The nature of my work is to give to other people, to nurture them. Most of the time this is fun and exhilarating, but only when I remember to nurture myself first.

By practicing the skill of self-communication, I have learned how my body feels when I am running on empty. First, my shoulders begin to tighten up. Then, if I am not paying attention, my arms begin to have irregular energy impulses, what some people might call the heebie-jeebies, and finally I feel as if I want to scream.

Before I understood how important it was to nurture myself on a continual basis, I let myself get to this point quite often. I have finally learned not to wait for the initial telltale signs of running on empty. Instead, I nurture myself as a part of my daily life.

As I continue to learn about nurturing, I have found the little everyday ways we care for ourselves are the most important. From the very beginning of my day until I sleep, and perhaps during sleep, I make sure to treat the most precious thing in my life—myself—with gentleness and kindness.

Learning to nurture myself on a daily basis has been a continuing process for me. I was raised to use time efficiently and expediently, which, of course, did not include self-indulgent behavior. However, self-nurturing is mandatory if I want to create a life-style honoring both the professional and personal aspects of my life. When I neglect myself, my ability to cope with the stress and tensions of the everyday world diminishes. My life is no longer in harmony; my ability to think and perceive is clearly reduced. I find it much more difficult to make wise, well thought-out life-directioning* decisions for myself on a moment-to-moment basis.

Each day is filled with a number of little ways we can nurture ourselves. For example, I find ways to nurture myself from the very beginning of my day. When I wake up, I stay in bed and give myself "ten more minutes" because I like to spend that drowsy, awakening time just with me. To make my morning even more hassle free, I take a leisurely shower and wash my hair at night so it is dry by morning. I also choose my clothes and lay them out the night before. Spending time both at night and in the morning being gentle and kind to my skin is also nurturing to me. The more I learn to love myself and nurture that self, the more I recognize what a precious and priceless commodity I am.

I have also found ways to nurture myself during my working day. I love challenge and variety and have created a career that allows me to stretch and grow. I schedule my work so I have whole days free and still accomplish everything on the days I do work. I have also created a work environment that nurtures me. My offices are warm and cozy, decorated in colors that make me feel peaceful. I enjoy keeping lots of my

---

*Language is a powerful thing. It is a tool we use to define who we are at any given moment. Dr. Timothy Leary said, "Words are a freezing of reality." Since our purpose here is *change*, it is sometimes necessary to create language that speaks to our changing needs. Like ourselves, words can develop, grow, and change to better describe our evolving thoughts, beliefs, attitudes, and feelings. Although *life-directioning* is not yet recognized as a word, it conveys what I want to express better than any existing word or words.

favorite things around the office too. I dress for comfort and almost never wear shoes, and my dog, Travis, is always there to add fun and love, sometimes at the most unexpected moments.

My favorite time is night. On my workdays, I schedule myself until ten or eleven at night. Then, when everyone is gone, and I feel the restful quiet of the night, I take care of the odds and ends required in running a business or a home. I like doing these chores at this hour because I feel unrushed and peaceful.

After I care for my personal needs and crawl into bed, the fun begins—I pick up the phone. Since most of my friends are also late-night people, we do our connecting around midnight. It is renewing and nurturing for me to sit in my cozy, comfortable bed, talking with the people I love.

When the talking is over and the night is truly quiet, I review my day. I read, or do my Homegrowth, or simply have wonderfully intimate conversations—with myself.

One of the most nurturing things I have ever done for myself is to create my home as a sanctuary. I have filled it with sounds, colors, light, and things that allow me to feel happy and harmonious; in fact, I even call my new home "Harmony."

The people who share my life, those I choose to allow into my sanctuary, are also nurturing to me. They surround me with love and laughter, but, beyond this, they give me the opportunity to learn how other, self-nurturing people live their lives. Perhaps there is only one thing in my life more nurturing than my friends—the love I am learning to have for myself and God/Goddess/All That Is.

Besides my daily activities, another important way I nurture myself is by attending workshops that add to my emotional and spiritual growth. The first thing I do every year is schedule the dates of workshops I plan to attend, usually one a month. This is my time of regeneration, of nurturing. Without it, I am not as productive or powerful as I am with it.

These workshops have helped me develop some very important skills, such as owning my personal power and providing myself with security and self-approval. If I provide myself with these essential needs, I do not feel compelled to secure a mate to provide them for me. This gives me the freedom to form intimate relationships on a clearer, more life-enhancing level.

Since I have begun to nurture myself, I am also a more nurturing person, softer and much gentler. And once again: When I develop a skill for myself—in this case nurturing—I can practice it with others.

In learning to communicate and share Jonathan's vulnerability, I was also developing these skills for myself. But when I realized how much he trusted me—allowing me to nurture him so intimately—I was catapulted to another new level of awareness. I needed to develop trust in order to reap all the benefits of nurturing and being nurtured.

Trust

Trust is the facet of intimacy missing in most of our lives. Like all the facets, trust and vulnerability are singularly essential in forming that gem called intimacy, yet they are also connected to each other. For it is impossible to trust without being *vulnerable*. Let's explore how these two facets of intimacy relate to each other.

When we trust, we agree to be vulnerable. By being vulnerable to me, Jonathan was willing to receive nurturing from me in ways he was not willing to accept from others. He also trusted me never to hurt him with the information he disclosed.

Every situation involving trust has four components.* To establish trust in any situation, all four components must be present. *Risk* is one of the components of trust. When we

*Lazaris, *The Synergy of Trust,* © 1981 NPN Publishing, Inc.

trust, we risk being *vulnerable*. Besides being a facet of intimacy, vulnerability is also another component of trust.

The next component of trust involves losses versus gains. When we trust, we are in the position to *lose much more than we could ultimately gain*. For instance, when Jonathan shared his secret with me, he took the risk of horrifying me to the extent of destroying our relationship. The only thing he had to gain was an understanding and compassionate ear. Clearly, he had more to lose than he had to gain.

The remaining component of trust is a difficult one for many of us. When we are genuinely trusting in any given situation, we honestly *expect to win*. We are fully cognizant of the risk we are taking, completely vulnerable to another human being, and we have no illusions about how much we have to lose; yet, from the very bottom of our hearts, we expect to win. When we trust, all four components are present.

Let's take a closer look at how this kind of trusting works. In the example I gave earlier, Jonathan *risked* a great deal by disclosing something that could end our relationship. He was *vulnerable*. He had much *more to lose than win* by taking this risk. Still, all the while, he *expected to win*, that is, he expected me not to betray his trust.

Expecting to win proved to be the most difficult component of trust for me. I was not willing to expect I could win. For instance, one of my main concerns with our relationship was the amount of time we spent together. I needed to spend more time with Jonathan. So I asked for more time together, taking pride in the fact that I had risked being vulnerable to him.

When Jonathan was not available to spend more time with me, I was hurt and angry. I had trusted him to respond favorably to my request. At least I thought I had. However, I learned I had not trusted at all.

Because I had learned long ago not to trust, I participated in an age-old game of self-deception. Instead of trusting Jonathan, I developed a skill that leads away from trust, away from intimacy. It is a skill in which too many of us have become proficient. I learned to substitute *testing* for trusting.

Trusting Versus Testing

Testing is not trusting, and the difference is consequential. We have already discussed the four components of trust (risking, being vulnerable, having more to lose than to win, and expecting to win). If even one component is missing, there is no trust. If we risk and are vulnerable but we have more to win than we have to lose, we are not trusting. If deep in our hearts, we never expect to win, we can never trust.

When I asked for more time with Jonathan, I risked asking for something he might refuse, and I was vulnerable. I fulfilled two components of trust—risk and vulnerability. But if Jonathan spent more time with me, I might gain more love and more intimacy, much more than I could ever lose.

Quite honestly, I never expected Jonathan to spend more time with me. Although I desperately wanted it, deep in my heart, I did not expect to win. Because I never honestly expected to win, I was testing his love. I wanted him to prove he loved me by spending more time with me. Unfortunately, this is not the only way we substitute testing for trusting.

Lack of honest communication can also lead to the testing game. Sometimes I was not clear and direct when I made my needs known to Jonathan. I would hint at what I wanted from him by pointing out the needs of other women or women in general. I said things such as, "Most of the women in my practice say they want more intimate communication from the men in their lives." I would expect him to get the message that *I* wanted more intimate communication in our relationship.

Then the test would come. Would Jonathan pick up my hint and communicate more intimately with me? Would he pass my test and prove his undying love and admiration of me? I'm sure the answers are quite apparent.

Testing can only create superficial relationships. Neverthe-less, trusting is so terrifying that many of us deny ourselves intimacy rather than develop trust. Like many of the other skills we have developed, learning to trust ourselves enables us to trust others. Learning to trust ourselves allows us to evaluate our growth and develop healthy relationships.

Loving

As we develop the components of lovingness discussed in Chapter Four, we take another step in our understanding of intimacy.

In a loving romantic relationship, it is important to real-ize that behavior we consider loving may not be interpreted by our partner as loving. One of the most loving questions we can ask our partner is, "What can I do so you feel more loved by me?" Most of us have never asked that question; yet it is one most of us would like to be asked.

Homegrowth 19: Loving Each Other

(1) If you are currently in a romantic relationship, sit down with your partner and agree to meet in one week. Schedule two separate sessions to discuss your answers to the question "What can I do so you feel more loved by me?"

→ One entire session should be devoted exclusively to each partner.

(2) Using the seven components of lovingness listed in Chapter Four (giving, responding, respect, knowing, humility, the courage to create, and caring), develop a list of things you consider to be loving. What can your partner do to make you feel more loved?

EXAMPLE:

Giving: I would like my partner to give me gifts reflecting his or her knowledge of me—gifts given with my happiness in mind.

Responding: I would like my partner to listen to what I say. I would like him or her to respond to my words and feelings rather than respond solely to his or her own feelings and words.

---

(3) Keep your list with you during the week so you can jot down ideas as they come to mind.

(4) Decide who would like to go first. Remember the entire session is exclusively devoted to that person's list.

(5) As you discuss each item on your list, have your partner interpret his or her understanding of your request. When you are satisfied that you have been understood, move to the next item on your list.

(6) Repeat steps 4 and 5 for the other partner on his or her designated day.

(7) Discuss how it felt to make the list, to share the information, and to hear your partner's requests.

Revealing these new awarenesses to our partner utilizes all the facets of intimacy we have learned to this point. When we communicate openly, we become vulnerable by exposing a new part of ourselves we have not shared before. To say, "I feel loved when you . . . ," is a very vulnerable place to be.

Listening, just as openly, to our partner's disclosures about our loving behavior also involves vulnerability. When we take our partner's needs into consideration and act upon them, our vulnerability can lead to nurturing. Allowing ourselves to be vulnerable—to be loved by our partner in ways we have shared—opens the door to nurturing.

Finally, learning how to communicate what makes us feel loved means we are trusting ourselves to create relationships that honor us. We give our partners the map to our heart, allowing them to impact us in the most positive ways. This kind of communication empowers us, our partners, and our relationships.

Learning to love our partners in ways that are acceptable to them is vital to a romantic relationship. For example, I knew one of Jonathan's greatest needs was to have a safe place, a sanctuary. He needed a place where he could be authentic, a place where he could talk openly about any number of personal topics without being censored. Because I wanted to love Jonathan in a way that he understood, I provided the sanctuary he needed whenever I could.

When we are loving to one another, we learn what makes us feel loved, and we share that with those we love. We can demonstrate our love in return by learning what they experience as loving.

Knowing

To know our true selves is to know love.

Kimberley Heart

Each of us is a complex, uniquely different conglomeration of simple basic elements. Intimacy is becoming more knowledgeable of our unique differences. Yet, for many of the reasons we have explored thus far, we have put walls between our self-knowing and our inner selves.

Perhaps the time has come to take down our walls and come to know the self we have kept hidden for so long. Throughout this book, we have been learning to explore and understand ourselves, from our own physicality, emotions, and needs to the very depths of our most hidden beliefs, attitudes, and thoughts.

One path toward self-knowledge is exploring where our feelings come from. Our knowledge of ourselves is incomplete without a sense of understanding why we feel the way we do. The following Homegrowth can be used to help you identify and understand why you feel the way you do. Use this Homegrowth any time you want to understand yourself better.

Homegrowth 20: Feeling the Feelings

(1) Choose any feeling you would like to explore further and answer the following questions.

What are the feelings I am experiencing?

→ It is important to identify and label the feelings we experience. Recognizing our feelings is the first clue to their origins.

Why now?

→ It is important that we ask ourselves these questions: "Why am I experiencing these feelings now?" "How is today different than yesterday?" "What has happened in my life that allows me to experience feelings I have denied up to this point?" Whatever has initiated these feelings now can be something as seemingly obscure as a dream or as concrete as a life crisis.

What growth has allowed me to deal with feelings I was previously unaware of?

→ It is important that we see new feelings as evidence of growth rather than an indication that something is wrong with us. Sometimes we experience new feelings because we have removed layers of emotional trash that were blocking these feelings, thus allowing the new feelings to surface.

What, where, and when would be the most obvious place to search for the roots of my current feelings?

→ For instance, if we have identified our feelings as sadness, based on our lack of deservability, it would make sense to look to our childhood for the origin of our lack of deservability.* Like an adult mystery game, it takes thought to find the most obvious place to begin.

(2) Once you have identified the most appropriate place to begin your search, experiment with the written technique discussed in Chapter Two in Homegrowth 3, You Are What You Believe. Or go to your safe place in meditation and let the child within come and talk with you and tell you his or her perspective. (See *Introducing the Child-Self* in the Meditations, Tapes, and Booklets section of the Bibliography.)

Identifying, exploring, and understanding our feelings gives us a fuller and clearer picture of who we are and why we are. Once we have found the origin of our current feelings, we can have a deeper and more profound connection with ourselves. This connection is what precipitates self-understanding. Understanding ourselves is the phenomenon of being connected with our pasts, our presents, and our possible futures via our thoughts, feelings, and intuition.

---

*Language is a powerful thing. It is a tool we use to define who we are at any given moment. Dr. Timothy Leary said, "Words are a freezing of reality." Since our purpose here is *change*, it is sometimes necessary to create language that speaks to our changing needs. Like ourselves, words can develop, grow, and change to better describe our evolving thoughts, beliefs, attitudes, and feelings. Although *deservability* is not yet recognized as a word, it conveys what I want to express better than any existing word or words.

The Intuitive Connection

Intimacy comes from daring to know another person; however, we can know another only to the degree that we dare to know ourselves. When we are willing to know even the hidden parts of ourselves, we can begin to know each other. One of the aspects about ourselves we have denied for too long is our intuition.

Sometimes, when we are in the midst of our search for self-knowledge, we experience something called a "hit" in the personal-growth vernacular. A "hit" is a seemingly unexplained wave of understanding that allows us insight into the current situation. For instance, sometimes when Jonathan and I were discussing his life, I would get a hit or spontaneous insight into the situation that was not accessible by cognitive thought alone.

The following story is an example of this sensation. One hot day in July, I mentioned to Jonathan that we were running behind schedule and needed to leave immediately if we were going to be on time for a dinner engagement. Jonathan's response was instantaneously startling. His angry reply was so inappropriate, I knew there was something important behind his knee-jerk response. He stormed around the house for a few minutes telling me not to "nag" him. As we were discussing his reflexive reaction, a sense of his ex-wife began to form in my mind.

Since this sensation refused to leave me, I said to him, "I got a hit that this has something to do with your ex-wife; could that be true?"

If I had ignored the information I received from my hit because I couldn't cognitively explain it, we would have focused on the trivial, superficial topic of my pushiness as Jonathan viewed the current situation. However, since I was comfortable with the information I knew instinctively—intuitively—we were able to reach a more accurate understanding of the situation. By reflecting on his feelings and his automatic response, coupled with the insight provided by my hit, we were able to determine that the present situation triggered old angers Jonathan had at his wife and even deeper old angers he still had not resolved with his mother.

Most of us continue to deny our hits or intuition simply because they frighten us. Because we do not understand where intuitive thoughts or feelings come from, we doubt whether they can be trusted. It is this fear of the unknown that keeps us from this very special and integral part of ourselves.

How often have we told ourselves too late, "I knew I should have done that, but I just didn't listen to myself"? As we become more knowing of our own self-systems, we learn to listen to our intuitive self, trusting our "inner voice." The time has come to integrate this internal guidance system we have discounted or ignored altogether.

Because intuition is revered and honored in many Asian cultures, Buddhist parents recognize such talent in their young children. In much the same way that Western parents send their children off to gymnastic centers to develop inborn athletic talents into skills, Buddhists send their intuitive children to monasteries, where priests facilitate the development of these raw spiritual talents into highly regarded and honored skills.

In our culture, however, intuition is demeaned as illogical and irrational. We not only believe, we demand, that everything have a logical, cognitive explanation. We have little tolerance for acknowledging the phenomenon of a paradox, viewing it only as a problem that must have a coherent solution. Because of this, we mask our intuition by using acceptable phrases such as business hunch, lucky guess, or gut feeling.

Learning to recognize, trust, and utilize this untapped human resource allows us a more intimate relationship with ourselves and with the special people in our lives.

Some examples of intuition in our day-to-day lives include:

Dreams that tell us what is to come. Many of us, at one time or another, have experienced this disturbing phenomenon. However, most of us tend to discount these dreams because we buy into the cultural mumbo jumbo that tells us we cannot prophesy, foretell, or predict the future. Yet, if we move beyond our fears and begin to pay attention to these dreams, we will learn how much wisdom they can bestow upon us.

Seeing pictures in our minds of what has happened although we were not present. For example, have you ever had a friend complain of a lost article, such as a set of keys? Instantly, a picture forms in your head, you can "see" exactly where the keys are—under a cushion, in the back of a drawer—but you say nothing. Weeks later, that same friend might mention finding the keys in the exact place you had pictured them.

Hearing sounds or voices from within ourselves that answer questions or offer guidance as our intuitive link. I often suggest to my clients who seem hopelessly lost in confusion, "Listen to the whispers." What else is more appropriate to trust under such circumstances than our own innate wisdom?

Sensing tactile feelings of another person's discomfort or pain is another form of intuition. For instance, when Jonathan was thinking of me, even when he was miles away, I experienced a sharp twinge in my right shoulder. The feelings always occurred in the exact same spot. Curious about this phenomenon, Jonathan began to document these experiences, noting the exact moment he was thinking of me. I kept similar records, noting the exact moment I experienced the twinge. The timing, we discovered, was usually within minutes—too close to call coincidental.

Smelling aromas—past or future. Though I have never experienced it, some of my clients have given me examples of olfactory precognition. One client often experiences the aroma of her mother's kitchen before receiving a phone call from her mother.

Because we have little understanding of intuition, we have developed little faith in it. I, too, had only a vague grasp of this powerful element of myself until a few years ago. I knew I was sensitive to other people's feelings, but I had never paid much attention to it. Sensitivity of this nature is socially acceptable intuition. We hear about it masked behind words such as *compassion* and *empathy*.

In my late twenties, however, I made a very interesting self-discovery about my sensitivity. I learned my body can accurately perceive another's physical pain. I was sitting in the lobby of a friend's office speaking with him. When a woman walked behind me and sat at the far side of the room, I immediately experienced a sharp, stabbing pain in my left kidney.

Somehow, I knew the pain I felt was not a reflection of my own physical well-being. Taking courage in hand, I walked over to the woman and said, "Excuse me, this is a very bizarre question, but are you having problems with your left kidney?"

Without missing a beat or even wondering how I knew, she said, "Yes. I have kidney stones and am in a lot of pain." At that point, I realized the capacity of my sensitivity.

At the same time, our sensitivity or intuitions should never become a burden. Learning when and how to use these talents is a skill. For example, like Buddhist children who are trained at an early age to monitor their intuition appropriately, I needed to learn to use my sensitivity in a way that was suitable for me.

For example, it would be a critical error on my part to experience my clients' feelings on an emotional or physical level. Overloaded with feelings not belonging to me, I would soon be susceptible to professional burnout. On a conscious level, I learned to open and close the door of my sensitivity, allowing the energy of others to permeate my body only at appropriate times.

Knowing more about the intricacies of ourselves is a process of allowing. Discovering our intuitive abilities is a matter of recognizing elements about ourselves that have always been there but have been ignored or suppressed because of misunderstanding, ignorance, or fear. Knowing ourselves is an engaging, exciting lifelong challenge. It takes focus, energy, and willingness.

Our willingness to know ourselves transmits the message that we consider ourselves worthy of attention and focus. In his book *The Undiscovered Self*, Carl Jung wrote about this very process: "If he (the client) follows through his intention (rigorous self-examination and self-knowledge), he will not only discover some important truths about himself, but will also have gained a psychological advantage, he will have succeeded in deeming himself worthy of serious attention and sympathetic interest" (chapter VI, p. 10).

Knowing ourselves, deeming ourselves worthy of serious attention, requires that we understand ourselves on both a cognitive and intuitive level. This process of self-knowledge—of learning who we are, what we want, and how we choose to live our lives—engenders the responsibility and freedom to create a life that fulfills our heart's desires.

Alan Watts described accurately the joys inherent in self-knowledge: "Self-knowledge leads to wonder, and wonder to curiosity and investigations so that nothing interests people more than people, even if only one's own person" (*The Book*, chapter VI, p. 120).

Courage

There is no first or last facet of intimacy; each facet is merely connected to and enhances the others. Courage, the one facet we have yet to explore, is integral in developing every facet of intimacy. It is the ability to act with heart and spirit in spite of our fears.

Courage is often misunderstood. Too many of us believe that *courage* means "without fear." This is not true. Courage is our willingness to act even though we are afraid.

Courage is a wondrous miracle of the human spirit. It means reaching down into our depths and finding that extra something that allows us to move beyond the limitations of our fears. That extra something is courage.

Developing intimacy can be a frightening process. If we are not afraid of one facet, we are usually afraid of another. However, as we develop courage, it becomes easier to develop the other facets of intimacy. Conversely, as we develop each of the others, we enhance our courage.

For each of us, courage is different. In many of my past relationships, I was willing to sacrifice intimacy in order to acquire "the man" at any cost. I was so afraid of being alone, unloved, and abandoned that I was willing to give up communicating to myself with meaningful information about my feelings. I refused to be vulnerable and allow myself access to my deepest self. Since I did not nurture myself, I expected my partner to do it for me. Trust was nonexistent, and my search for self-knowing was hampered by my fear of what I might find.

Still, because I was *willing* to have a warm, loving, caring, *intimate* relationship, I courageously began to take baby steps toward true intimacy with myself, and then with the special people in my life.

This is how courage works. It grows little by little, each tiny step taking us along at the pace that is right for us.

The Blue Sapphire

Each facet of intimacy builds upon and is enhanced by all the others. Ultimately, as in any synergistic system, the facets of intimacy culminate to form the complete gem we have been describing throughout this section.

When we remain conscious of each facet and how it intensifies the entire relationship, we can learn to create an intimate relationship.

Intimacy is a priceless gem, a wonder created by our ability to connect and bond with ourselves and other human beings. As we practice the skills that create genuine intimacy, continuing to change the beliefs about intimacy that inhibit our lives, we will be able to reap the rewards a truly intimate relationship has to offer.

The following Homegrowth is designed to increase your awareness of both the quantity and quality of intimacy you currently have in your life.

Homegrowth 21: What's Your I.Q. (Intimacy Quotient)?

(1) Down the left-hand side of a sheet of paper, list all of the people you consider to be intimate friends.

(2) Across the top of the paper, write the seven facets of an intimate relationship:

Communication
Vulnerability
Nurturing
Trust
Loving
Knowing
Courage

→ You should now have seven columns for each intimate friend on your list.

(3) In each column, honestly rate your level of intimacy with each friend on a scale of 1 to 10, 10 being the highest level of intimacy.

EXAMPLE:
You might rate communication with your best friend as 10, vulnerability as 7, and so forth.

---

(4) For each column that did not receive a 10, notice what was missing.

→ Even if you rated someone 9 for any category, notice why.

EXAMPLE:
If you rank your best friend as 7 in the vulnerability category, it might be because you withhold your feelings when you are angry at her or him.

→ By noticing why you are not as vulnerable as you might be, you can begin to remedy the situation if you choose.

(5) When you have completed each individual evaluation, add the seven numbers to reach a final score for your intimacy level with each friend.

(6) As you review all of your scores, you might notice certain patterns.

→ All your vulnerability scores might be 5 or less. This would indicate a need to work on your beliefs, attitudes, and feelings concerning vulnerability.

→ Your communication scores might all be 9 and above. You will want to notice and take pleasure in your success with this facet of intimacy.

Over time, as you repeat this Homegrowth, notice how your levels of intimacy become deeper. As you become more aware and more adept at intimacy, your Intimacy Quotient will increase.

As you develop more intimacy in your life, however, your scores might dip. This interesting phenomenon occurs because your scoring criteria have become more sophisticated. That is, once you know more about intimacy, you will expect more from yourself. This is partly a reflection of your growth. It is also indicative of the infinite quality of intimacy. Since intimacy is always evolving, growing, and unfolding, there is always more intimacy available to you.

Taking a closer look at my Intimacy Quotient allowed me to notice I had not achieved the type of intimacy I wanted with the people who were special in my life. Since true intimacy was lacking in my life, I soon discovered it required a commitment not only of courage but of time and energy.

Because we have chosen to live in a world bordered by time, we also have limited the number of intimate relationships we can maintain at one time. The fact is, we simply do not have enough time to consciously create all the facets of intimacy with more than four people at one time. That is correct. Four is the maximum number of intimate relationships any one human being can create and maintain at one time. Most of us, however, can consider ourselves quite proficient if we can manage one or two intimate relationships.

Roadblocks on the Path to Intimacy

While it is true that our willingness to learn the skills of intimacy can create the relationships we want, sometimes we build emotional blockages that keep us from the intimacy we say we want.

We all have walls of unresolved feelings standing in our

paths blocking our passages toward intimate relationships. Now is the time to discover which emotional blockages we have used to limit our ability to be intimate. The following section delineates some of the major blockages to intimacy.

Martyrdom and Superindependence

Martyrdom and superindependent behavior are two blocks you and I have probably used at one time or another to keep us from intimacy. Both martyrs and superindependent people have a high need to control others. Martyrs do this by "giving until it hurts." Superindependent people do this by "going it alone."

Martyrs are easily recognizable once you know what to look for. The fact is, every one of us has been a martyr at one time or another. Martyrs feel misunderstood and unappreciated. They silently suffer their lot in life, and have little understanding of their impact on others. They see themselves as the person who is being hurt and accept no responsibility for their dilemmas or for their impact.

For instance, my Great-Aunt Louise was forever demonstrating how much she did for us and how much she suffered through her giving. Her unspoken yet clear message was that because she suffered for us, she was a wonderful person, and thus it was our duty to appreciate her many sacrifices.

There is another type of martyr you will probably recognize as well. These are the long-suffering silent types who sigh a lot. They encourage you to take from them while at the same time they give you a silent message: If you do take what they proffer, they will have nothing left, but it's okay because you are worth more than they.

There is a popular T.V. commercial that epitomizes this type of martyr. A woman faces the screen offering us her last goodie, saying, "Go ahead, take the last one. I don't really need it. Really, it's okay." All the while, she is looking at us with doe eyes that are pleading with us to take from her. Then she can justify her feelings of being used and unappreciated.

Martyrs are grand manipulators. They use guilt, pity, coercion, and anything else they can dream up in order to control the people in their lives. At the same time, they appear to be giving, kind, selfless human beings. Their motto is "Poor me, I've been misunderstood again."

Martyrs are dangerous because they usually end up hurting everyone. They harm themselves by failing to honor their own needs, and they injure others through their manipulation and installation of guilt. They use guilt to control, continuing the cycle of abusive behavior.

We can recognize when we have been with a martyr by the "not-enough" feelings or feelings of unexplained anger we experience after interacting with one.

It is easy to see how martyrs have the ability to hurt those around them. Their behavior is not the harmless product of old age or selfless giving. It is mean, destructive, and insidious. The insidiousness comes from the guilt they ply us with. How could we possibly be angry or hurt by their manipulations when they do so much for so many? Because we buy into this manipulation, and often do it ourselves, we refuse to recognize how destructive this behavior is.

Because we fear intimacy, we may use martyrdom to protect ourselves from it. Martyrdom excludes the possibility of intimacy because none of the facets can exist within an environment of pity, coercion, manipulation, or any other device used to control.

On the other hand, superindependent people do not ask anything of anyone, ever. Their motto is, "I can do it myself." They are self-sufficient characters who carry independence to the point of isolation. Superindependent people attempt to control their environment by eliminating any interference or input that might confuse their well-orchestrated world.

Because superindependent people also attempt to control

everything around them, they cut themselves off from nurturing, trust, and all of the other facets of intimacy. For instance, superindependent people rarely ask for help, for to do so would expose their vulnerability.

As I mentioned before, after my rebirthing session, I discovered that very early in life that I decided not to depend on others. During my adolescence, I molded this belief into: "I should not depend on others and am a better person if I do not."

I spent most of my twenties not asking for help, especially when I needed it most desperately. I camouflaged the pain of a child who could not trust or depend on the adults around her with a hardened young adult who refused to be vulnerable or nurtured. If I had asked for help, I would have seen the wounded child within me.

Being superindependent is not what our culture has led us to believe; it is not worthy of the praise society is willing to give it. Superindependence is nothing short of destructive because it severs us from our very core, robbing us of intimacy.

Superindependent people cannot afford to develop the facets of intimacy because they are too busy trying to survive according to the rules of society. These rules forbid weakness, sentimentality, and especially intimacy. Consequently, we attempt to attain emotional fulfillment through superficial achievements such as high-paying jobs, trophies, and big houses. This leaves us emotionally destitute. All of our achievements have left us without the one essential, an authentic connection with ourselves and with another human being.

When we choose to hide behind either of these disguises, martyrdom or superindependence, we close ourselves off from any opportunity to form intimate relationships.

Projecting the Past Onto the Present

Projecting the past onto the present is another psychological block to intimacy. Most of us drag around the balls and chains of our unresolved feelings about our parents, past lovers, teachers, and so on. Unresolved feelings grossly inhibit our ability to perceive current relationships accurately. When we project our feelings about people from our past onto the people in our present, we build a huge wall between ourselves and an intimate relationship.

Whenever a situation arises that triggers a subconscious memory of the past (and such situations arise more frequently than you and I care to imagine), we reflexively react to the memories, not the current situation. This psychological trigger or stimulus can move our behavior and feelings into an automatic mode.

When we are functioning from this position, there is no prethought or conscious decision making. It is very much like the physical reflexes we can elicit from our bodies simply by striking the right physical trigger such as the knee-jerk reflex.

For instance, the story I have already related about Jonathan's knee-jerk reaction when I mentioned we needed to leave soon if we were to be on time for our engagement is an example of triggering subconscious memories. Ultimately, we learned I had stimulated or triggered something in him that subconsciously reminded him of his ex-wife. His reaction was frustration and rage. By simply suggesting that we needed to leave soon, I had unknowingly pushed a psychological trigger.

Knowing that unresolved feelings from past relationships cause direct impact in our current experiences gives us motivation to finish with the past. Resolving the past is essential if we are to create intimacy.

Homegrowth 22: The Beginning of Resolution

(1) On the left-hand side of a piece of paper, list the people for whom you have unresolved feelings.

(2) On the right-hand side of the paper, list the feeling(s) that remain unresolved in connection to each person on the list.

EXAMPLE:	
Jane	anger
Mother	hurt, anger
Father	resentment
teacher	hate

(3) Complete the Payoff Questions from Homegrowth 8, Exploring the Why, in Chapter Three to gain insight into your refusal to let go of your past.

(4) List the reasons you discovered from completing the Payoff Questions for refusing to resolve your feelings.

(5) Using the information you have learned in this book, evaluate each situation you have allowed to remain unresolved.

→ Determine whether this unresolved feeling came from a sense of victimhood or from a sense of personal power.

→ If you determine that victimhood was the motivating feeling, what new skills and personal insights have you gained to make this nonproductive attempt to protect yourself no longer necessary?

EXAMPLE:

Jane:

• If I released my anger, I am afraid I might allow her to be close to me and she will hurt me again.

• These old feelings of anger come from a sense of victimhood.

• I do not have to continue a relationship with anyone who continually hurts me. I have the right to accept or reject any relationship offered to me. If I stay angry at Jane, I hurt myself, not Jane. I do not have to use anger to protect myself.

• I have choices, and these choices give me power.

Fear of Intimacy

Fear of intimacy is the third psychological block to an intimate relationship. If any of the seven facets of intimacy frighten us, fear of intimacy as a whole becomes an issue for us. Most of us are afraid of at least one facet. By determining what facet(s) we fear and the reasons for our fear, we can resolve the fear.

All of us need to understand and face our fears. Denied fear is not only destructive; it can also be immobilizing. Perhaps a more realistic definition of fear will make it easier for us to face.

There are two clear, concise definitions of fear that I like. The first is: Fear is a missing piece of information. The second is: F.E.A.R.—False Evidence Appearing Real.

The missing piece of information is synonymous with our fear of the unknown. This fear is so intense, it can control our lives by creating a mental fog through which we perceive the world. This fog prevents us from seeing situations and people in a clear, accurate fashion. Consequently, we often refrain from decision making and have little or no concept of our choices. For example, entering darkened rooms, meeting strangers, and flying in airplanes are experiences with missing pieces of information that elicit fear for some.

But fear can be even more insidious. Many of us stay in relationships we no longer want because of one or more missing pieces of information. For example, we might fear not knowing what the future holds. Perhaps we do not know that we can take care of ourselves. Or we do not trust ourselves to create another, more fulfilling relationship. Missing pieces of information will immobilize us if we allow them to.

The second definition of fear that I like is: F.E.A.R.—False Evidence Appearing Real. False evidence is a product of faulty belief systems. If our belief systems are inaccurate, they will produce evidence that reinforces inaccurate or faulty perceptions.

For example, your lover has not called in three days and has not returned your messages. You become frightened that (1) something is physically wrong with her or him; (2) she or he is leaving you and this is her or his way of indicating that; or (3) she or he has already run off with someone else. Each circumstance is a hypothesis based simply on the sole fact that your partner has not called in three days.

More often than not, we reach out and grasp the worst scenario and begin to ruminate on the evidence. Before long, what was once a simple fact is distorted into false evidence. This false evidence is mutated in our minds into something that appears real. Before long, we are consumed in fear that rules our perceptions.

When your lover returns, she or he may mention leaving a message on your machine saying she or he would be gone for four days and would call when she or he returned. You suddenly remember the rainstorm that turned your electricity off and erased all of your messages. Unfortunately, in your fear, you were unable to see anything but the false evidence.

Examining the causes of our fears will help us learn what parts of ourselves we are trying to protect. For example, if as vulnerable children, we were manipulated and hurt, we will believe the false evidence that our vulnerability caused us to be hurt. Therefore, we might decide not to be vulnerable simply to protect ourselves from being hurt again.

As adults, never questioning our fear of vulnerability, the false evidence obtained in childhood continues to dictate our present behavior; we do not allow ourselves the gift of our own vulnerability.

By understanding our fears, we can fill in the missing pieces of information or begin to correct the faulty belief system. When we notice what frightens us, we can do something about it. Living with fear that we never conceptualize is sentencing ourselves to an undeterminable amount of unhappy years.

Homegrowth 23: Understanding Fear

(1) On the left-hand side of a piece of paper, list all seven facets of intimacy:

Communication
Vulnerability
Nurturing
Trust
Loving
Knowing
Courage

(2) On the right-hand side, list the reasons you might fear that facet of intimacy.

→ If trust is the facet of intimacy most frightening for you, you might list childhood experiences that facilitated and enhanced your belief that people cannot be trusted.

EXAMPLE:
Trust:
- My dad did not come home and spend time with me when he promised he would. He always had a good reason, but the truth was he lied to me.
- I listened to my parents lie on the phone to their friends and relatives, and I believed that if they would lie to their friends, they would lie to me.
- My mom lied, making excuses why my dad was never around when I needed him for father-daughter night, school plays, or bedtime.

(3) Now turn your attention to your behavior in the last year and note the situations where you continued your childhood belief that people cannot be trusted.

EXAMPLE:

Trust:

From the above list, I can see that I learned people lie and cannot be trusted. I see that I do not believe what people say to me; I always look for evidence to prove that they are telling me the truth. I have insulted several of my friends by not believing what they have told me. I push people away by not being able to trust.

(4) Determine what definition most appropriately defines the fear you have identified.

(5) Repeat this procedure for every facet of intimacy.

The objective of this Homegrowth is to help you determine several important points. First of all, it will help you realize if you are, indeed, afraid of intimacy, and if you are, which facets you consider most frightening. Second, you will gain some insight into why these facets are frightening. What piece of information do you need in order to become more comfortable with the facets that frighten you? Third, you will be able to discern what faulty evidence or beliefs you continue to hold onto that are diminishing your ability to have the relationship you say you want. Finally, this Homegrowth will help you determine if you are using the past and the accumulated fears of yesterday to inhibit your ability to be intimate today.

Noticing what category your fears fall under gives you a good start in clearing them up. If most of your fears fall under a missing piece of information, supply yourself with that missing information. Begin to trust yourself to handle any situation in a way that honors you—even if all the information is not yet available to you.

If most of your fears fall under False Evidence Appearing Real, then do what I call a reality check. Check out if your perceptions of people and situations are accurate. In each frightening situation, take the time to ask yourself, "Am I perceiving the situation accurately or am I projecting past fear onto my present?" Another way of asking the same question is, "What facts do I know?" "What am I assuming?" Remember, false evidence moves us out of our center.

Completing the Circle

The only thing that one really knows about human nature is that it changes.

Oscar Wilde

During our exploration of intimacy, we have utilized the UnlimitedGrowth process outlined in Chapter Two. We are ready to complete the final step of permanent *Change.*

1. We have become more aware of ourselves and thus more attuned to noticing.
2. (a) We have worked with the Payoff Questions to help us recognize where we hold ourselves back and why.
   (b) We have noticed and taken responsibility for the impact of our behavior both on ourselves and on others.
3. We have forgiven ourselves.
4. And, finally, we will open the door to changing any aspect of our life by completing Meditation 2, Changing Your Beliefs, as part of the next Homegrowth.

Remember, you are worth every bit of work it has taken to reach this final step. So, with gentleness and kindness, take that last step—now.

Homegrowth 24: Intimacy and UnlimitedGrowth

(1) Definitively state the belief about intimacy you want to change and write it on a piece of paper.

> EXAMPLE:
> It is not safe to trust.

(2) Complete the first part of Step Two of UnlimitedGrowth.

→ Understanding: Write your answers to the Payoff Questions in Homegrowth 8, Exploring the Why, in Chapter Three, for the facet of intimacy you have chosen.

> EXAMPLE:
> • What do I avoid by not trusting my lover?
> • What righteous feelings(s) am I hanging onto by not trusting?

(3) After you have completed the Payoff Questions, write about how this behavior impacts you, your relationship, and those around you.

> EXAMPLE:
> • My lack of trust impacts my relationship because I with-hold my feelings. This decreases our ability to have meaningful communication. My lack of trust diminishes my willingness to nurture and to be nurtured. It clearly rules out vulnerability.
> • I am impacted because I do not trust myself enough to believe I have chosen a partner worthy of my trust and consequently, my relationship is not fulfilling.
> • My partner is impacted by not being trusted, which creates separation and pain.

(4) Complete the second part of the second step by accepting responsibility for the impact you just wrote about.

(5) Complete the third step in UnlimitedGrowth, Meditation 1, Finally Free, found in the Meditation Appendix. Forgive yourself

for having the feelings that kept you from the intimacy you wanted. If you need a refresher on self-forgiveness, refer to Chapter Three. (6) Write the belief you wish to change once again.

EXAMPLE:
It is not safe to trust.

---

(7) Write the new belief you wish to hold.

EXAMPLE:
It is safe to trust myself.

---

(8) Initiate Meditation 2, Changing Beliefs, found in the Meditation Appendix.

After you have completed the Homegrowths in this chapter, you will be able to change any beliefs you have. This includes any beliefs concerning intimacy that are not working for you.

An Unexpected Gift

As I reviewed all I had learned about intimacy, I realized I had expected to achieve closer, more intimate relationships—and I did. However, I also gained one very important and unexpected benefit—the realization that I could not create intimacy with Jonathan, or anyone else, until I created intimacy with myself. All of my work led me to a more intimate relationship with myself.

I was learning to communicate with myself more openly and with a deeper level of meaning. Slowly, I became vulnerable enough to allow myself to gently probe the parts of me I had kept secret for so long. I learned to nurture myself, to take care of the most precious person in my life. At the same time, my level of self-trust rose as I handled myself with care and respect.

Soon, I found that loving myself is an activity that captures my total awareness and demands my energy. The process of searching for intimacy allowed me the courage to continue my exploration into the depths of myself and the world around me.

Intimacy Versus Sex

An intimate relationship can be created with anyone—not only with a lover. Look back over Homegrowth 21, What's Your I.Q. (Intimacy Quotient)?, and notice how many of the intimate relationships in your life are also sexual relationships. Now review the seven facets of intimacy and notice that the facets of this deep blue sapphire we call intimacy never included sex. Nowhere in discussing communication, vulnerability, nurturing, trust, loving, knowing, and courage have we even hinted at sex or sexuality.

Too often, you and I hear the word *intimacy* and immediately equate it with sexuality. In fact, in our culture, *sex* and *intimacy* have almost become synonymous; yet, there is nothing genuinely intimate about sex, unless we add the facets of intimacy to the sexual experience.

The truth is, choosing to have sex with someone before some degree of intimacy outside of the bedroom has been established can severely hamper intimacy in the bedroom.

In Chapter Seven, we will discover how we can create the *magic* of intimate sex.

Chapter Seven
Sex: A Double Rainbow

One recent rainy afternoon, while maneuvering my car around a particularly curvy on-ramp to the freeway, I experienced a rare phenomenon of nature. Deep in thought about this chapter on sex, I wondered how would I ever find the words to convey the wonder and mystery of sex.

As I drove, I could see a blue sky with the sun shining radiantly in the east, while in the west, a dark mist engulfed the skies. I was right in the middle—the line of demarcation. At that precise moment, I glanced toward the east once more and saw the rays of the sun doing a dance—a magic dance—with glistening raindrops. The result? The first complete double rainbow I have ever seen. From horizon to horizon, the hues of red, orange, yellow, green, blue, and purple cascaded downward.

Though this may sound unbelievable, especially for a southern California freeway, the traffic actually slowed while the drivers shared in this spectacle of nature.

As for myself, I will never forget that afternoon. There, under that extraordinary double rainbow, I experienced an ethereal connection with something I cannot quite explain, even now. At that precise moment, I realized that the inherent power of sex was like the commanding beauty of a double rainbow and the ethereal connection I was experiencing.

In its own mysterious way, sex magically allows us to transcend ourselves, and to connect in a spiritual partnership with God/Goddess/All That Is. It is a masterful creation woven together by the mystery and the magic that enhances our very spirituality.

When it comes to sex, I find it wonderfully fascinating that we have duped ourselves into believing we know how to "do it." We also believe we can teach others how to "do it" with us. If, by chance, we have any doubts whatsoever, there are myriad books available on the subject of "how-to."

This is not one of those books. Instead, this chapter deals with creating the magical experience of sex—that elusive double rainbow.

Dominion Versus Domination

Before we delve into the depths of the mystery and the magic that comprise sex, let's consider the topic of *power*, since that is precisely how we, as human beings, have come to view not only sex but our sexuality as well.

The fact is, we have not erred. Sex is inherently powerful. However, if we are going to learn to utilize and celebrate that power to honor our integrity and further our connection with God/Goddess/All That Is, it is necessary to understand power itself, specifically the concepts of dominion and domination.

Simply stated, *dominion* is personal power from within, while *domination* is outward control or power over something or someone.

Domination is an action that speaks to our insecurities and resultant neediness to have control over our surroundings including our relationships. It is an authoritarian force born of our fears and feeds upon our lack of self-trust.

When we do not trust ourselves to make appropriate life-directioning decisions, we cannot trust anyone else. We begin to feel helpless and powerless and our need to take control over our environment increases. We believe that the only way we can be safe is to decide what is appropriate for everyone else.

We act out of domination every time we think our lovers should agree with and meet our needs as if they were their own. For example, if we decide when, where, and how often we should have sex without considering the other's needs, we are dominating the sexual relationship. Every time we manipulate or coerce anyone with the potential loss of love or security, we are acting out of domination. Domination is a desperate act of powerlessness that arises from our feelings of fear, anger, and helplessness.

Dominion, on the other hand, is a state of being. It is the ability and willingness to act. It is not the action itself. Dominion comes from within the self when we are one with or in tune with ourselves. It is born in our ability to trust ourselves, and it grows with our competence, honoring our personal excellence and integrity. When we are in dominion, we reflect our self-trust, self-respect, self-esteem, and self-confidence. Because these self-skills allow us to direction our own lives, our need to manipulate or control our environment diminishes.

In trusting that we will meet our own needs, we trust that those we love will also take care of their own needs first. Dominion is knowing that we alone preside over our own life-directioning power.

Dominion is genuine wisdom empowered with gentleness, courage, insight, and ingenuity. In other words, dominion is true personal power. Every time we tell our loved ones, "I love you. Go, do, be what you are for you, and we will remain connected," clearly we are in a state of dominion.

Clues From the Past

In order to gain another perspective on how dominion versus domination has affected our attitudes on sex, a look backward might be helpful. Clearly, a detailed history of sex would take up volumes. The roles of culture, politics, and religion in such an account would be far too complex and intricate to address in a few short pages. However, I would like to guide you on a mystical minitrip into time. Perhaps if we go back far enough, we will find an age when everyone shared in the *magic* of sex, long before its power became shrouded in the mystery.

Long ago the ways of the Goddess taught that responsibility for one's life resided with the individual; each had dominion over her or his own life, including sex and sexuality. As we begin to explore the various aspects of sex, we will learn more about dominion, the Goddess, and how her ways are beginning to enlighten us once again. Perhaps if we look closely, we may learn how the powerful *magic* of sex became a mystery in the first place.

A Heart-Felt Theory of Sexual Evolution, or Who's on Top?

Once upon a time, when the Queen of Heaven guided the planet, it has been said that the sexual union between people was simply natural and appropriate. Both women and men chose to use their bodies, minds, and spirits in ways that were personally pleasing, honoring, and without restriction. Sex was not a function of control or power over, but a shared experience, honoring both. Such were the ways of the Goddess— offering dominion, not domination.

In the temples of the Goddess, priestesses used sex as a means of healing, nurturing, and celebrating life. This was considered one of their holiest and most sacred duties. For one year, each woman would serve in the temple as a priestess. During this time, she would bond with the energy of the Goddess. When she left the temple, she would carry that energy with her, spreading the joy of life and the celebration of love with those around her.

Children born to priestesses during their service to the Goddess were considered sacred children. They were cared for and loved by the entire community. It was unthinkable that these children were owned by or belonged to anyone.

In the time of the Goddess, symbols of domination such as ownership of women, children, or land were nonexistent. In those days, women as well as men were taught to be whole within themselves. Though interpersonal relationships were important, the self was never sacrificed for the good of another or the good of the group.

An independent woman with dominion over her own life was called *virgin*. Long before the term became polluted, *virgin* meant a woman who was, thought, and acted autonomously, in her own right—a woman whole unto herself. People were committed to the care and nurturing of themselves and each other simply because it honored them and consequently the Goddess.

The people of this age understood the inherent power of sex. For example, an ill person was often placed in a room where a couple shared physical lovemaking, to be nurtured by the healing power generated by the physical sharing of love. It was known that the body, mind, and spirit could restore itself more fervently in an atmosphere of shared love.

In like manner, the energy created by two people sharing themselves in love was considered to be powerful enough to fertilize a field before planting. If a farmer wanted his field blessed before the planting season, for example, he knew enough to make love upon it. If any aspect of life needed regenerating, one would dedicate the lovemaking experience to that aspect of life. It was common knowledge that sex was regenerative and restorative. Perhaps the time has come for us to regain some of this primal knowledge.

The body itself was also highly revered by these *ancient ones*. For instance, vaginal secretions were considered to be holy fluids. In the temples of the Goddess, blood that flowed from a woman during her moon cycle, known as "red wine," was consecrated long before the Bible referred to lamb's blood as sacred to God. Vaginal secretions, often called "white wine," were taken internally and considered to be rejuvenating. These sacred fluids were available to all for enhancing and prolonging life. Time has a way of distorting knowledge and wisdom. Over eons of time, people forgot this power lay within themselves. Ritual took the place of what was once natural, life-enhancing power. Before long, even the purpose of the ritual was forgotten or distorted.

There are a number of fascinating books available on the Goddess and Her reemergence. You will find some listed in the Bibliography.

As time passed, for reasons that still remain hidden, the energy of the planet began to shift. Some feel this shift noted the beginnings of patriarchy or a dominator society. It is difficult to find the precise moment when things change, when beliefs become erroneous—for this is the essence of evolution. Such changes are slow and gradual, yet very certain.

The days of the Goddess were numbered. Her temples came under attack and were pillaged, Her priestesses raped. What was once sacred, was defiled. Priestesses who healed and nurtured others were called witches and whores; even their sacred children were desecrated and termed bastards. What once gave light, became lost in the darkness of fear. Ultimately, sex became a religious and political pawn, albeit a powerful one.

As this planetary energy shift became more and more pronounced, people began to lose connection with the essence of themselves and began mistrusting their own personal power. As they disconnected from themselves as the source of their own power, they also lost their connection with the Goddess. Gradually, as personal power was given up and eventually denied, domination superseded dominion; control and power over became rules of the day.

The belief in private ownership of land emerged. Along with that, a new concept of marriage materialized, dictating that women and children should become the property of men. To the ancients, marriage was simply a celebration of the oneness created through physical lovemaking. However, as organized religion and politics became more and more powerful, marriage became a signed contract of ownership, giving a man the right to a woman's person and property. Again, what was once sacred became defiled.

As domination continued to sprawl throughout the land, religion and politics merged into nearly the same force, a force that would eventually wield ultimate control over everyone. Perhaps due to fear instigated by the misunderstanding of the energy shift, people began handing over their personal rights and responsibilities—one by one—to a belief in control and domination. It is important to remember that power can never be taken from a human being; it must be given up.

These new political and religious beliefs presupposed that the profound personal power of sex would also need to be controlled in order to maintain a sense of dominance. If sex was indeed as powerful as was suspected, then the practice of sex—the private activities of men and women—needed to be controlled as well.

It was no longer acceptable for people to reach within themselves to touch the Goddess. In fact, it became blasphemy to even think that two beings together could create the type of power and magic that is inherent in the sexual union.

For political reasons, then, it became the duty of organized religion to dictate laws authorizing that the sexual union be condoned only between a man and his wife and only for the purpose of procreation. Limiting sex to such a joyless, powerless act camouflaged its true power and essence from the participants.

It was at this point in time that people began to lose sight of the *magic.* They willingly forgot that sex is one way human beings answer their natural call to connect with themselves, others, and the Goddess. When people gave up this natural connection with the Goddess, there was no recourse but to search outside themselves for that connection. Because they gave up their personal power and self-responsibility, it became easy to believe the lie: Only those in authority could provide the connection that is inherently individual.

Sadly, people forgot that it is never possible for one human being to provide a connection with the All That Is for another. That drive or call to connect is universally shared, yet it must be answered individually.

The people gave their authority figures prestige, control, and riches as payment for attempting to create this impossible connection. Because they had abandoned their connection with self, they allowed their beautiful and natural need to connect with the ultimate love source, God/Goddess/All That Is, to be exploited and preyed upon.

As the millennia have passed, our belief that we should dominate the world totally blocked the fact that dominion ever existed. Instead we chose to believe that control and power over was always the "natural" way of things. We also began to believe the physical act of sex was nothing more than a momentary physical connection—one that usually causes us more guilt and pain than joy and light.

In the depths of us, however, we know that most of us live our lives and share our love in ways that are distorted and disempowering. Perhaps this knowledge alone has placed us on the verge of another planetary shift. For we have allowed a vague awareness of this truth to seep into our conscious mind, creating a magical mystery. This is a mystery that we must solve if we are to create life filled with dominion and sex filled with *magic*.

The Mystery of Sex

You and I both know that there are scientific explanations for rainbows—even double rainbows. Nevertheless, how we feel when we experience them often remains a mystery. So it is with sex. We consider ourselves to be knowledgeable and sophisticated when it comes to sex. Yet we only guess and wonder at its hidden power. As we discussed above, when two people share emotional and physical love, they can create a bonding that is beyond themselves and reaches to touch God/ Goddess/All That Is—a spiritual connection far beyond words. In order to regain what our ancestors unwittingly gave up, we have cunningly created a mystery of what was once *magic*. It will remain a mystery only until we awaken to the memory that we ourselves are personally responsible for that bonding. It is our job to follow the clues and put the pieces together. Only then, can we regain our birthright.

The Game Is Afoot

Like any good mystery, searching for the true essence of sex has led us down many a dark alley, following elusive clues that seem to lead only to one more dead-end. There are questions with no answers and, just as often, answers to questions we have not yet thought of.

Because so many of us have chosen similar windings paths and dead-end alleys to solve this mystery of sex, I will share a brief summary of my own exploration of the mystery of sex with you.

When I was in high school, I remember reading the Kama Sutra, the Kinsey Report, and everything else about sex I could get my hands on. I was eager to learn about this thing everyone did but nobody ever talked about.

Because sex was so interesting to me, I often fantasized what my first sexual experience should be like. When I was a senior in high school, I moved into my own apartment and began dating a young man who was a few years older and more sexually experienced than I. At that time, I consciously decided that this young man would be my first sexual partner and that our first sexual experience would be the day I graduated from high school. Together, we spent hours talking about the parameters of my first sexual experience.

Somehow, in my adolescent mind, I had decided that if I was a great lover, I would be worthy of love. The only way I knew to be worthy of love was to understand and achieve excellence in my sexual performance. Therefore, I was committed to learning all I could about man-woman coupling.

Even after all my planning, on graduation day I was still frightened and not in touch with how I felt. The only thing I knew for certain was that I would achieve my goal.

Of course, we had the logistics down pat. Since we would have more privacy, we decided that his house was the most appropriate place and that afternoon was the best time. I remember pacing up and down my living room watching out the window for him to come and get me. My roommates were home and commented on my skittishness. When he finally came, I ran out to the car, slammed the door, and said, "Let's go!" I was so frightened that he asked me if I wanted to postpone our plans. I replied, "I just want to get it over with." Much to my surprise, this outraged him. When we got to his house, we went to his room, locked the bedroom door, and began.

When the deed was done, I remember smiling to myself, not out of pleasure or out of a feeling of closeness with this man, but because I had accomplished my goal. It was over. I was no longer a virgin, yet for some unknown reason, the mystery remained. Though I now had some experience, I had come no closer to understanding the mystery of sex. And I still did not feel worthy of love.

At that point in my exploration of the mystery of sex, I continued to believe that if I could learn to be a wonderful and exciting lover, I would be worth loving. If I could learn everything there was to know about pleasing a man in bed, then I would never be left or abandoned. Certainly now that I had experienced sex, gaining expertise would unravel the mystery of sex for me.

I failed to notice, however, that I had reached the dead-end of a blind alley. I had based my deservability to be loved on my sexual performance—on how much pleasure I could give my lover. I never questioned the fact that my pleasure was not all it could be. I had no time for such concerns; I was busy sleuthing! What I was unable to see with my limited knowledge and experience was that I was following the wrong clues, chasing a red herring.

By the time I graduated from college, my interest in sex had not waned. I had gained what I considered to be sexual prowess and even became arrogant in my attitudes about my sexual performance. However, even though I knew more didactic information about sex than most people, I still had a feeling that I was missing something. I began to realize that maybe the mystery I was trying to solve had nothing to do with securing love or deservability. I began to get a vague idea that *all* I had been doing was chasing red herrings. Once more, trying to put myself on the right track, I took every available course on human sexuality. In physician's assistant school, I chose to take a rotation with a team of sex therapists who had been trained by Masters and Johnson. Now I would get the real scoop. Now I was on my way to solving the mystery by becoming a sex expert.

By the time I completed P.A. school, I knew the anatomy and physiology of sex as well as how to treat the symptomatology of sexual dysfunction. Yes, I knew it all—or so I thought. Then one day, I realized that no matter how much I knew, there was still one more class I wanted to take, one more book I needed to read. Why? Because all the pieces still did not come together.

Playing Sherlock to my current partner's Watson, I began to explore a new trail. Perhaps this one will also look familiar to you. It sounded quite logical to deduce that if something was missing, there must, indeed, be more. Elementary! But, more what? Simply more sex? Maybe more intense sex? Or perhaps more orgasms? With my partner, I explored the various avenues of physical sex. Together, we experimented with a wide assortment of positions, locations, and devices. But this trail, too, led to a dead-end. Something was still missing.

By this point, I had intellectual data as well as empirical evidence. Even after all this time, there was still a voice within me that nagged me to look deeper. Skill and knowledge simply were not enough. I began to realize that sex was a larger mystery than I had ever dreamed. Yet, I simply did not know how much larger.

Along with my therapist license came more classes, more books; and I began to learn more about the human psyche. Well into this adventure of discovering the mystery of sex, I began to understand more clearly the intricate and closely woven tapestry between physical performance, emotional acceptance, and intellectual understanding. I began to wonder if these components were in fact the foundation for understanding the mystery of sex.

I was looking for an answer to a question that still was not specific enough to ask. I was looking for something to quiet the voice within me—a voice that insisted sex held more *magic* and power than had been unveiled at this point in my journey.

With each new discovery—whether it was a physical discovery of how the mechanics of sex worked or an understanding of the emotional connections that happen during sex—one phenomenon repeated itself. I learned more about myself. What began as a journey to solve the mystery of sex and consequently secure the love of a man became a journey into myself, securing a connection with me. It became more and more clear that sex was not just a fulfilling physical and emotional experience, it was a secret passage into the depths of me and—if I chose—into the depths of the person with whom I shared the sexual experience.

Unlocking the Mystery

Solving the mystery was a revelation. Discovering that sex opened a passageway into myself and answered the question "Who am I?" was only one of the mysteries to be solved. There were actually three mysteries—three mysteries that, when solved, exploded into *magic.*

These mysteries can be summed up by asking three questions: "Who am I?" "Who are you?" "What can we create together?" Because of this revelation, another door would eventually be opened to me—a doorway into the depths of God/Goddess/All That Is.

When I looked back at my sexual history, I saw that there was a common denominator to all my experiences: I looked to my lover to provide me with the answers to my questions. This should not have come as a surprise to me, but it did. Even after all my growth, I would occasionally still look to a man to give me what I refused to provide for myself. In this particular journey into the mysteries of sex, my refusal to assess and meet my own needs often led to an emptiness I did not understand.

By this time, I knew a tremendous amount about sex and I was willing to share all I knew with my lovers, yet the emptiness that consumed me after "good sex" continued to be my nemesis.

Hidden Agendas

I have often wondered why sometimes sex just does not work. We have all experienced sex that should have been satisfying, yet it only left us feeling empty and alone. I remember times lying next to Jonathan after having what could be described as explosive physical sex, and yet I felt like crying. Why? I would look over at Jonathan and wonder what happened or what had not happened to make me feel so alone inside. This remained a mystery until I heard a lecture called *The Magick of Sex*.*

As I listened, the pieces to the puzzle of why I sometimes felt lonely after sex began to fit together. In order for sex to be emotionally as well as physically bonding, partners must enter the sexual experience with matching agendas. That is, each partner must want something from the sexual experience that is mutually compatible with the other's desires.

For instance, if my reason for making love with Jonathan was to secure his love, and his reason for making love with me was to have fun, exciting sex, our agendas clearly were noncompatible. When agendas do not match, a schism is formed and, rather than bonding, a separation is forged. Consequently, we feel separated and lonely.

Although I never had the courage to ask Jonathan if he felt the emptiness as well, it makes sense that if I felt withdrawn and empty, I would not be emotionally nurturing to him. It would follow that he would experience some level of disconnection as well.

This phenomenon of matched agendas is so powerful that even agendas that are considered socially unacceptable can still create a bonding and satisfying sexual experience—if they match. For instance, a person who wants to have sex to dominate another can match agendas with someone who wants to have sex in order to be dominated. This type of matched agendas will create sexual experiences that work. This phenomenon is the reason why sadists match themselves with masochists to create sex that works for them individually. Conversely, two sadists or two masochists will find difficulty creating a satisfying sexual experience because their agendas do not match.

Who Am I? Who Are You?

The process of answering the question "Who am I?" can

*Lazaris, *The Magick of Sex*, © 1981 NPN Publishing, Inc.

enable us to match our agendas with our partner's. One of the many ways we can learn about ourselves is to explore our true agendas for having sex. We can explore our agendas by honestly communicating with ourselves. For example, the true answers may not be readily available when we ask ourselves the question "Why am I sharing sex with my partner and why am I doing it now?"

However, as we continue to observe ourselves before, during, and after sex, we can begin to get a fuller picture of our needs, wants, and desires for having sex.

There are innumerable agendas for having sex. For instance, sometimes we may want sex simply for the attention, or perhaps we might want an outside source of validation—someone to express how beautiful or sexy we are. There might be other occasions when we are angry and want to use sex to punish our partner or even ourselves. Maybe we are feeling an overwhelming love for our partner that words alone cannot convey, so we choose to communicate our love physically. It might well be that we are simply bored and want sex to move us beyond our boredom.

After exploring our agendas, we can share them openly and honestly with our partners. How we share our agendas can vary as drastically as our agendas themselves. For example, we might kiss our partner on the neck and whisper in her or his ear, "I'm really horny and want you right now." The message is that we want to have a physically fun, sexual experience. When our partner knows our agenda, she or he can choose to match it or perhaps decide to pass on the offer for the time being.

At a time when we might be feeling lonely and our agenda is to be reassured we are loved, we might invite our partner into the sexual experience by telling him or her, "I'm feeling lonely, I need to feel close to you and need you to share your love with me." Again, our partner has the right and responsibility to choose consciously whether her or his agenda could match our own to create a satisfying experience. This quality of honest sharing helps us discover more about ourselves by paying attention to which agendas we feel uncomfortable sharing and which agendas seem fun and exciting to share. Knowing and exploring our discomfort and our excitement unveils more of who we are. Our partner in turn will reveal more of her or himself to us through the same process. When we are open to our lover's agendas, we can more readily match our agendas with his or hers. Matching agendas with our partner's is the foundation for creating exciting, fulfilling sex.

If this process of matching agendas sounds familiar, it is. When we explore, share, and match our agendas for having sex with our partners, we are simply using the skills we learned in Chapter Six, Intimacy. We are communicating with meaning, we are vulnerable, we are trusting ourselves and our partner, we are willing to share what we know about ourselves, and to demonstrate the courage to do all of the above.

Homegrowth 25: Matched Pair

(1) On a piece of paper, answer the following questions about your last three sexual experiences.

- The reason (my agenda) I chose to share in the sexual experience is _____ .
- The reason (agenda) I think my partner shared the experience was _____ .
- Using a scale of 1 to 10, answer the following questions:
  I left the experience with what level of emotional fulfillment?
  I left the experience with what level of physical fulfillment?
- I left the experience feeling closer to my partner. Y/N
  If not, why not?
  If yes, how and why did I feel closer?

- I left the experience feeling better about myself. Y/N
  If not, why not?
  If yes, why?

EXAMPLE:

My agenda for having sex was that I did not want to disappoint my partner, who indicated a desire for the experience.
My partner's agenda was to satisfy a physical desire.
Emotional fulfillment: 5
Physical fulfillment: 7
No, I did not feel closer to my partner because, in this experience, we did not share emotional closeness as we usually do, and I missed that.
I did not feel better about myself because I did not do anything to enhance the emotional closeness I missed.

---

(2) After reviewing your answers for all three sexual experiences, summarize any patterns you have discovered.

EXAMPLE:

After reviewing my answers, it is apparent that I want to be an active participant in creating my sexual experiences. When I am, my agendas are clear to my partner, and I leave the experience feeling better about the relationship and myself.

---

(3) If you are currently in a relationship, have your partner complete steps 1 and 2 and discuss your realizations with each other. You can use the following issues to initiate your discussion.

- Share your agendas for having sex.
- Were you aware of your partner's true agendas for having sex?
- How do you feel about each other's agendas?
- Do your agendas match?

- Do your fulfillment levels match?
- If your agendas are not compatible, talk about how you can change this.

Discovering our hidden agendas allows us to discover more about ourselves, our partners, and what sex has to reveal to us about ourselves. The wealth of information unveiled during this learning process allows us to ask the questions "Who are you?" and "What can we create together?"

We can begin to discover the intricacies and power of "What can we create together?" by first understanding the Law of Resonance.

The Law of Resonance

Physicists tell us that everything in the Universe is in constant motion or vibration; that includes you and me. We are simply vibratory forces. Each of the cells in our bodies vibrates at a particular rate; in turn, each individual organ within us vibrates at a rate unique to that organ. All these vibrations combine to form a symphony that equals you or me.

As we unveil the mysteries of sex, it is important to understand that one of the reasons we are not always in harmony with each other is because each of us vibrates at a unique rate. For example, I may be vibrating in a light, happy mood like Mozart's "Eine Kleine Nachtmusik" and my friend might be vibrating at a heavy, depressed mood, like Mozart's "Requiem." When the two of us come together, there is a clash. The two masterpieces cannot be played side by side and create harmony. Something must change, which brings us to the Law of Resonance.

The Law of Resonance states that when one vibrating body is exposed to a similar body, eventually the vibration of one body will reinforce that of the other. In other words, when two similar vibrating forces come together, they will eventually vibrate at the same, or nearly the same, rate. For example, if I am light and happy and spend time with my friend who is depressed, the Law of Resonance says that the two of us will eventually begin to vibrate at the same or close to the same frequency.

It is important to know that we have several options, taking this law of physics into consideration. In the above example, for instance, I can hold my resonance and consequently my friend's vibratory frequency will be reinforced to match mine. Or, my friend can hold his vibratory level at a stronger frequency and my feelings of lightness and happiness will move closer to his depression. A third option is to meet somewhere between both frequencies. Still another option is to leave the situation entirely, thereby canceling the chance of being affected by someone else's resonance.

If we become conscious of our own moods or vibratory levels, we can use the Law of Resonance to our advantage. Becoming conscious of our moods means noticing what kind of mood we are in—sad, happy, withdrawn, and so forth—at any given moment.

For instance, when I first became aware of the Law of Resonance, I began to pay close attention to my interactions with Jonathan. Since I often liked to explore Jonathan's feelings instead of my own, this was a healthy exercise for me because I had to focus on my own feelings instead of Jonathan's. As I became more conscious of my own awareness, sensations, and responses, I soon learned that this Law of Resonance could give me still another insight into the mystery "Who am I?"

We can become even more consciously aware of our level of resonance in most situations if we learn to tune our vibratory rates to the resonance of the Universe. Then, like finely crafted instruments, we can continue to re-tune on a daily basis.

Playing in Tune With the Universe

Tuning our resonance is done by matching our vibratory rates to the same frequency as those emitted by the colors of the rainbow. Throughout our bodies, there are centers of energy called chakras. The ancients matched these chakras with specific colors of the spectrum. The harmonic resonance of each position can be reproduced and enhanced by the vibratory frequency of the color matched to that position.

The following Homegrowth introduces the technique of tuning your chakras.

Homegrowth 26: In Tune With the Universe*

(1) Sit in a comfortable position, relax, and become attuned to your body.

(2) Imagine a blood red ruby at your first chakra, which is located in the center of your body at the level of your coccyx bone.

(3) Visualize the ruby spinning vertically as if it were a top. Spin it in any direction that feels right to you.

→ Allow the color red to permeate your entire being.

(4) Repeat this process for each of the remaining six chakras, using the following chart for the appropriate colors, position, gems, and functions of the seven chakras.

First Chakra
- Red
- Located in the center of the body at the level of the coccyx bone
- Ruby
- Center of security

Second Chakra
- Orange
- Located in the center of the body between a woman's ovaries or a man's testes

*Lazaris, *Mysterious Power of Chakras*, © 1986 NPN Publishing, Inc.

- Orange topaz (color of California poppies)
- Center of sexuality, pleasure, creativity, and compassion

Third Chakra
- Yellow
- Located two fingers above the navel
- Yellow Sapphire
- Center of all feelings other than love

Fourth Chakra
- Emerald Green
- Located between the sternum and the notch in your throat
- Emerald
- Center of love

Fifth Chakra
- Blue
- Located in center of throat
- Sapphire
- Center of communication and intimacy

Sixth Chakra
- Indigo
- Located behind the third eye at the root of your nose
- Deep Purple Amethyst
- Center of intuition, perception, and psychic awareness

Seventh Chakra
- White
- Located in the middle of your head
- Diamond
- Center of spirituality

(5) Visualizing the appropriate color spinning is all there is to tuning any chakra in your body: Focus on that chakra, visualize a gem and color coordinated to the vibratory rate of the chakra, spin the gem to retune the energy, and radiate it throughout the body.

When we take the time to spin our chakras each morning, we attune ourselves to the Universe. The benefits of this tuning will soon become apparent, as our days progress more smoothly and our moods become more honoring of us. By taking responsibility to set our resonance each day, we enhance our personal empowerment.

Our resonance is a powerful source of change. In order to be a source of change that honors us, we are helped by an awareness not only of our resonance, but also of the resonance or mood of the people we are with. Giving ourselves at least that much information, we can decide whether or not any given situation is healthy and honoring of us.

As we have already seen, our resonance can impact others as readily as theirs can impact us. When we allow other people's resonance to impact us in ways that honor us, we are using the Law of Resonance to our benefit.

When we allow other people's resonance to pull us away from ourselves and the knowledge of what honors us, we are giving a piece of our personal power away. It is important to assess each situation and determine if we are willing to move to the resonance of those around us, or if it is to our benefit to hold our own resonance.

I remember meeting Jonathan for lunch one day, consciously aware that I was cheery and excited to be with him. From the moment we met outside the restaurant, I sensed that he was angry and had no intentions of letting go of that anger. Halfway through lunch, I had knots in my stomach and could not wait to finish and get away from Jonathan. As I drove home alone, I recognized just how much conscious mental initiative I would need to hold my resonance at a level that served me and did not turn my power over to someone else. In any situation, we can learn to consciously hold those levels of resonance that honor us. Holding our resonance becomes easier by our increased awareness and by reinforcing our resonance with daily tuning.

Comprehending and using the Law of Resonance adds to our personal power and helps us take a deeper look into the question "What can we create together?" We can take this law into consideration whenever we spend time with other people. Before we enter important meetings, personal encounters, or even social gatherings, we can remind ourselves that our resonance can influence the entire tone of any situation. The Law of Resonance wakes us up to our personal power and allows us the clarity to be responsible for maintaining a resonance that works for us.

Finely Tuning the Relationship

Since the Law of Resonance is operative in our intimate relationships, we can learn to tune the resonance of the relationship. Just as we use our chakras and the colors of the spectrum to tune our personal resonance, there is a technique to bond more intimately with our partners. In fact, this technique can help partners match resonances so successfully that they can become aware of each other's thoughts.

Before beginning the following Homegrowth discuss with your partner your hesitations and excitement about taking another step in intimacy. Your work on intimacy will make this exercise much more rewarding.

Homegrowth 27: Spiritual Bonding*

(1) Lie down comfortably, close your eyes, and still your mind and body. Ask your partner to do the same. Be close enough to touch, but do not touch.

→ Both people do the following exercise simultaneously, without verbal or visual communication.

→ The key to this technique is to focus on giving to your partner, not on receiving.

*This exercise is based on a conversation with Lazaris.

(2) Begin by imagining a red beam of light generating from your red chakra. This beam of light will come out the back of your body, up over your head, softly flowing over the head of your partner and into the back of her or his body, settling at her or his red chakra.

→ Continue to pump red energy—security—from your body into your partner's until you feel you are finished.

→ Trust yourself to know when it is time to move on.

→ Your partner will be moving at his or her own rate; it need not match yours.

(3) When you are ready, without words, move your focus to your orange, or "pleasure and compassion," chakra and allow a flowing arched beam of orange light to flow out of the front of your body into the front of your partner's orange chakra.

→ Use arched beams of light in this technique.

→ When you have finished giving your partner the pleasure that is orange, turn your focus to your yellow chakra.

(4) From your yellow chakra, send an arched beam of yellow light out the front of your body into your partner's.

→ You are sending your partner an essence of all your feelings other than love.

(5) Both people continue to repeat this technique with each chakra at the individual paces until both have finished.

→ As we have discussed before, green is the color of love, blue is the color of communication and integrity, indigo is the color of intuition and psychic awareness, and white is the color of spirituality.

(6) When you have finished, quietly open your eyes and wait for your partner to open hers or his.

(7) Share with each other the experience of giving.

→ Was any one color easier to give? Which one? Which feelings are associated with that chakra? Was any color difficult to give? Was any beam of light less powerful? What feelings are associated with this chakra and is this something you have difficulty sharing in the relationship in general?

As time passes, it will become clear what you have given and what you have received. Traits that were once stronger in your partner will become stronger in you and vice versa. For instance, if your partner was the primary communicator in the relationship, by sharing her or his light with you, you can become more willing to communicate. The shared focused energy that is the heart of this technique aligns your resonance with your partner's in a way that honors you, your partner, and the relationship.

It amazes me that a process that is this easy can enhance a relationship in so many ways. Though the process is "easy," its power and significance is complex and far-reaching. Only when you experience the bonding in your relationship that was not probable before will you begin to understand the magnitude of this "easy" process.

Sex and the Law of Resonance

The Law of Resonance can also help us solve the mystery "What can we create together?" As we have already observed, the Law of Resonance explains how all of us constantly impact each other. All the effects of the Law of Resonance that we have already discussed are magnified during sex because of the unusual amount of energy released. In other words, the Law of Resonance combines with sexual energy exponentially to increase the amount of energy that impacts you and your partner during a sexual encounter:

$$(\text{The Law of Resonance} + \text{Sexual Energy})^n = \text{Powerful Impact}$$

This combined energy is so intense, that unless we are aware of our own resonance as well as that of our partner, we could be unknowingly impacted.

The power of this impact during sex can result in acquiring our partner's resonance and carrying it with us for as long as three weeks. For example, when we make love with a positive, enthusiastic person, we will pick up and carry some of that energy for up to three weeks. It also holds true that when we make love with a depressed, controlling person, we will carry some of that energy. Clearly, the level of personal responsibility in choosing our sexual partners increases in the same ratio as the level of impact.

The Law of Resonance gives us more clarity in discovering the answers to the three mysteries of sex—"Who am I?" "Who are you?" and "What can we create together?" The Law of Resonance enables us to have a clearer understanding of ourselves, the people around us, and how we impact each other. This level of conscious awareness adds to our personal empowerment. It also unveils another level of empowerment. By being consciously aware of our own state of well-being, we can choose to share that state with another. We can choose to become healers.

Sex as Healer

Long ago, during the time of the Goddess, it was known that sex could heal. Today, The Law of Resonance justifies this ancient knowledge. We can consciously choose to use the Law of Resonance to help heal our sexual partners.

This phenomenon became a reality for me one weekend when Jonathan and I were in the mountains. I was bombarded with all the symptoms of the flu and at the same time felt guilty and angry because I was responsible for what I thought would be a ruined weekend. Jonathan, however, had a different fantasy of our weekend. He consciously chose to focus his energy as a healing agent rather than a pleasure agent. So, when he crawled into bed with me, his intent was to use his energy and his body to help me heal myself. He held his resonance of a healthy, positive person with such integrity that I found it easy to match his energy. When I awoke the next morning, I felt much better and, by the end of the day, my level of physical and emotional health had moved to match his. This movement from a place of illness toward a place of wellness is called healing.

Each one of us can choose to facilitate emotional, physical, and spiritual healing in each other. The Law of Resonance enables us to utilize our own inherent powers of healing to help one another.

The more we understand about ourselves and how we fit into the scheme of things, the more imperative it is for us to be conscious of what we do. The Law of Resonance demonstrates this more clearly than any issue we have spoken to thus far. We impact ourselves and the world around us by our very existence. We can determine what that impact is only if we choose to be conscious of what we feel, what we do, what we say, and what we think, more and more of the time.

Synergy

"What can we create together?" The answer to this mystery has remained hidden in the mundane. For too long, we have accepted answers such as, "Together we can create children, better living conditions, security, happiness, and so forth." But you and I know that these things are not the *magic* we have been searching for. Inherently, we know there is more to what we can create together sexually. Humans have been held in bondage by our society, religion, and politics to the extent that we have been afraid to even glimpse the *magic* of sex.

However, now that we have developed tools to explore the

mysteries of sex, we no longer need succumb to the immobilizing fear. We can create a possibility that was not available to us before, by answering the questions "Who am I?" and "Who are you?" Armed with a greater understanding of ourselves, each other, and what we can create together, we now have the power to step boldly out of the dark mystery of sex into the magical light. We can finally celebrate sex as it was meant to be, cascading around us in all the colors of the rainbow.

The *Magic* of Sex

Understanding the Mystery in the *Magic*

What is this *magic* I have been in search of and why does a part of me instinctively know I can create it in my life? I suppose all of us, at some very base and primitive level, know that there is so much more to life here on the planet than we have already experienced. Yet, we seem baffled as to exactly what we have been missing. We yearn for this *magic* in the depths of our souls. Somehow, at the very core of our beings, we carry the memory that we were given the right and means to connect with the very source of all creation. Yet, we find ourselves immobilized when it comes to any practical pursuit of this elusive and mysterious *magic* that can add purpose, power, beauty, and dignity to our lives.

The dictionary defines *magic* as "any mysterious, seemingly inexplicable, or extraordinary power or influence." For me, the *magic* of sex means creating more than we ever believed possible. Somewhere in the depths of myself, I know it is possible (though it seems inexplicable) to truly become one with the All That Is. As we discussed in the previous section, how to create this kind of *magic* was lost to us, its only legacy is the mystery we are driven to solve. Since I, too, did not know how to explain or create this extraordinary power I knew was inherently mine, I turned once again to *The Magick of Sex.* *

To Put Asunder

It never ceases to amaze me how everything in the Universe is connected. Today, biologists, physicists, and especially nuclear physicists are becoming profoundly aware of this universal connectedness. *Fission* and *fusion* are terms used by both biologists and nuclear physicists to explain concepts from reproduction to nuclear energy. For example, fission is the nuclear theory behind the atom bomb, while fusion is the theory behind the hydrogen bomb. Let's go a step further, and connect the principles of fission and fusion to explain the power of sex.

Fission is as different from fusion as empty sex is from soul-satisfying sex because fission creates energy by splitting. The energy created by fusion, however, is released when two wholes fuse together to form a complete new entity.

Before we explore the intricacies of fusion, let's take a deeper look at simple fission, much as a nuclear physicist might. In the center of every atom is a nucleus where most of the mass and energy of the atom is stored. Fission describes the splitting apart or separating of that nucleus, resulting in a vast release of energy and a reduction in the size of the original nucleus. In physics, fission is a two-step process: the splitting of the nucleus and the resultant release of energy. If we take this process a step further, we can see how it might also describe some of our sexual encounters. When you and I create sexual fission with our partner, we come together as a single nucleus but we retain our original separateness—never bonding or forming something new. The release of energy called orgasm, which can accompany this coming together (intercourse), serves only to seal our individual separateness.

*Lazaris, *The Magick of Sex*, © 1981 NPN Publishing, Inc.

We end up moving away from each other feeling emptier or less than we did before. This is sexual fission.

We have already discussed the dynamics of empty sex and the hidden agendas that perpetuate our loneliness. If we imagine ourselves as nuclei and our hidden agendas as nonpermeable borders that surround us, it becomes easier to understand why and how we would create fission in our sexual encounters.

To Touch the Face of God

As strongly as fission creates energy by separating, fusion unites so powerfully that an entirely new entity is created. This new creation generates an unimaginable magnitude of energy. In physics, fusion is a three-step process. The first step in fusion involves the merging of two nuclei. The creation of more than what was present before they merge is the second step of fusion. The energy released by the creation of this new mass is the third step in fusion.

In our sexual relationships, fusion teaches us how to reach beyond. Cryptically concealed in this phenomenon is the power to catapult us beyond the mere physical pleasures of sex. The magic was right in front of us all the time, like the "Purloined Letter," so close that we could not see.

When we create sexual fusion, we allow our spirits to merge, creating an energy too great to be contained by the boundaries of our physical bodies. The vast energy of our combined spirits allows us to soar beyond all time and space "to touch the face of God."

The power inherent in sexual fusion can change us for all time. It can re-create us anew, alive with the spirit of All That Is. When we create sexual fusion, we not only merge our individual spirits with the one we love, we actually merge with a part of God/Goddess/All That Is. We become one with each other and the All That Is. This loving connection is one way we—as human beings—can create ultimate *magic* in our lives here on the planet. This, gentle lovers, is our birthright, one of the reasons we are here.

Creating the *Magic*

How do we create this ultimate *magic*? To begin with, creating fusion is not a matter of following a cookbook "how-to." Creating fusion involves an attitude and a willingness, an understanding and a belief that this type of connection is possible.

The all-important third step in fusion—becoming one with the All That Is—is the *magic*. Obviously, this powerful interaction is not merely a physical process. In sexual relationships, most of us can get from A to Z in an infinite number of ways and still end up empty. It is certain that sexual positions alone do not create *magic*, nor does simply understanding the erogenous zones of our bodies. And believe it or not, creating the *magic* does not include having the best-looking body on the beach or by the pool. While all these things might be important to personal aesthetics, they do not begin to comprise the *magic*.

No, the *magic* lies in our own individual willingness to create something beyond basic physical pleasure. This is not quite as simplistic as it sounds. To be willing to create something as magical as fusion with a sexual partner—a lover—means risking total surrender, total vulnerability. If these two words leave us a bit shaky, perhaps we have not completely comprehended their meanings.

Surrendering Is Not Giving Up—It's Getting More

In our society, many equate vulnerability with weakness. Surrender has come to mean defeat, failure, not enough—all without honor. Unfortunately, we have forgotten the power unleashed by total surrender.

Surrender is the precursor to vulnerability. In order to become vulnerable, we must surrender our control. This means giving up the limiting factors of control, manipulation, and debilitating fear. Surrendering is the conscious act of releasing our defenses and agreeing to be totally vulnerable to the impact our lovers have upon us.

Because the power of surrender is so great, many of us are afraid to let go. The fear of letting go has caused many of us to be preorgasmic, which is to say we have not yet allowed ourselves to experience orgasm. Others who have at one time been orgasmic have become frightened by loss of control and consequently have become nonorgasmic.

We have willingly given up the pleasure of orgasm because we fear total surrender. Yet without total surrender, we are powerless to create orgasm. More important, we are also powerless to create fusion—our connection with another human being that will form a new magical bond intensified by the All That Is.

If experiencing orgasm requires surrendering in our sexual relationship, then I would suggest that creating the *magic* of sexual fusion *demands* surrender; for in the surrendering is the vulnerability, and consequently the power. Only this mutual surrender—allowing total vulnerability—can carry us beyond physical pleasure into the spiritual realm of the *magic* of sex.

The Spirituality of Sex

As human beings, we are all spiritual entities. This is not to say we must believe in or practice any formal religion, for our spirituality is much more complex than religion alone. Spirituality is our own personal connection with the source of all creation, with the All That Is.

When we create fusion, we touch the All That Is in a way that enhances and changes our connection with ourselves and with God/Goddess/All That Is forever. Consequently, sex can be one avenue leading to a more profound and loving connection with God/Goddess/All That Is.

Perhaps now you can understand why the *magic* of sex is so very much like that double rainbow I saw one unforgettable rainy afternoon. Certainly, I could describe the mechanics of a double rainbow for you. I could discuss the rain and the angle of the sun's rays; I could speak about refractions, reflections, and spectrums. But will you really ever know what it *feels* like to experience a double rainbow until you actually do? So it is with sexual fusion. Until you experience total surrender with a partner who wants the very same thing, you will only wonder, guess, and speculate about the *magic* of sex.

True, double rainbows are a rare phenomenon of nature. But creating fusion, or the *magic* of sex, does not need to be. Let's take a look at why we don't create fusion more often in our sexual relationships.

Roadblocks to Fusion

The roadblocks to fusion are much the same as the blockages to intimacy we discussed in Chapter Six, Intimacy. Just as with intimacy, I found it difficult to understand why I wouldn't want to create fusion in my sexual relationships. However, after I began to identify my blockages to fusion, it became clear why I had not allowed myself to create it.

Fear

In spite of our fears, you and I are seekers. We know this about each other because we have come this far in our exploration of relationships together. We know now that our fears are not impassable.

As we mentioned in our discussion of fear, our fears are diverse and often intermingled. We can fear the unknown, we can fear surrender, we can fear being vulnerable, and we can also fear our impact. Many of us are also frightened of the intensity of our emotions. We are afraid of how deeply we can love and consequently how badly we can be hurt. We may fear the enormity of our rage and consequently limit our capacity for tenderness. We limit the scope of one emotion with the penalty of limiting the scope of all our emotions.

There are people who have never heard of the word *fusion;* yet they create it consistently because their fears do not block their way. My fears, however, did get in my way. Like many of you, I was frightened by the intensity of my emotions. I loved Jonathan so much, I feared how vulnerable this left me. My fear blocked creating fusion with Jonathan.

Understanding some of my fears and dealing with them made it easier for me to be *willing* to create fusion in my relationships. Remember how important willingness is. If we want to create fusion, we must first be willing.

Knowing what frightened me helped. If I was afraid of the intensity of my emotions, the intense feelings involved in a relationship that created fusion were just as frightening.

Deservability

Our inability to accept total happiness also blocks fusion. If we do not believe we deserve happiness, we will not create sexual fusion. Some of us might believe we deserve a degree of pleasure. We even allow ourselves to enjoy sex as a wonderful physical experience. But how willing are we to allow total pleasure that is not only physical and emotional, but spiritual as well?

Sadly, most of us believe total pleasure is something we must earn. The fact is, we deserve total happiness solely by virtue of our birth. Unless we accept this, we might not allow ourselves this type of intense, magical sex.

Victimhood

When we choose victimhood, we deny any opportunity to create fusion in our relationships. As victims, we cannot consider creating fusion. The *magic* of fusion would eliminate our ability to rationalize our position as less than everyone else. Victimhood is a choice that limits our joys and fulfillment in life.

Searching for Validation

If we use our sexual experiences to gain validation from our sexual partners, we will not allow fusion. When our agenda is to gain validation of our womanhood or manhood, worth, or esteem, we cannot create sexual fusion.

Child Versus Adult

The creation of fusion in a relationship demands that we operate from our adult self. If our behavior is constantly based on the needs of our child self, we forfeit the possibility of fusion. When we want our lovers to meet our needs, we cannot maintain the level of responsibility inherent in the creation of fusion.

Lack of Monogamy

In the beginning, when we are creating an intimate, romantic, sexual relationship, I believe it is wise to choose sexual monogamy. Monogamy facilitates a level of intimacy that allows surrender and encourages vulnerability. Once this level of intimacy is created, monogamy usually becomes a natural choice.

The combined forces of intimacy and monogamy facilitate fusion. Monogamy allows a level of focus that enhances and magnifies the power of each facet of intimacy. Together, intimacy and monogamy create a powerful source of energy that can result in fusion.

In fact, I will go one step further. I strongly believe that monogamy is necessary in the creation of fusion. Dividing our energy and focus with more than one partner dilutes our power and precludes the possibility of fusion.

The psychological blockages to fusion can be dismantled if we notice what is in our way. Acknowledging our blockages and understanding how we can move beyond them are big steps in our personal growth. If this sounds familiar, it is because this is simply another view of UnlimitedGrowth, the change process we have been exploring in Homegrowths throughout this book.

Homegrowth 28: Dismantling the Blockages

(1) Step One: *Notice* the psychological blockages you wish to change.

(a) Write the single blockage you wish to change.

> EXAMPLE:
> My intense feelings are dangerous.

(2) Step Two: *Acknowledge* your blockages.

a. *Understand* what your payoffs are. To do this, write answers to the Payoff Questions from Homegrowth 8, Exploring the Why, in Chapter 3.
b. Accept responsibility for their *impact* on yourself and others. Write about your impact on yourself and others.

(3) Step Three: *Forgive* yourself. To do this, complete Meditation 1, Finally Free, found in the Meditation Appendix.

(4) Step Four: *Change* the belief(s) the psychological blockage is based on.

EXAMPLE:
The fear of your intense emotions might be recorded in your subconscious mind as
"My intense feelings are dangerous."

You can change this belief to
"My intense feelings are life enhancing."

Complete Meditation 2, Changing Your Beliefs, found in the Meditation Appendix.

UnlimitedGrowth works as well in creating fusion as it does in facilitating intimacy.

The Journey Is Its Own Reward

As we have learned along the way, although fusion might be our goal, there are many other things we can create together—some of them delightful in and of themselves. However, sometimes when we are in a hurry to get to our destination, we often ignore the journey. In reaching fusion, as with many other goals, the journey has much to offer.

Although I was in search of the *magic* of sex, I did not want to miss any wonderful sights along the way. So, I began examining some positive sexual encounters we can create together—even before we get to the *magic*.

For example, we can experience a simple exchange of physical pleasure. We can experience this pleasure whenever we share the same agenda as our partners. Or perhaps we want to create a sexual encounter to promote healing. Either we or our partners can help heal or be healed. Still another example of a positive sexual encounter is a loving, sharing, emotionally fulfilling experience that can honestly be called lovemaking.

Making Love*

As I learned about lovemaking, I noticed I had been ignoring the best parts of the journey. Making love can be a bonding, exhilarating experience that can create a depth of wealth and knowledge all on its own.

In truth, genuine lovemaking is also a path—resplendent with passion, honor, and respect—that can lead to fusion and the *magic* of sex.

Homegrowth 29: Creating the *Magic*

We have traveled long and far together, gathering skills, tools, and raw materials necessary to create the romantic relationship we have always dreamed of. Now we have reached the part of our journey where we are able to consciously make some significant internal decisions for ourselves.

In the following section, we will explore some explicit physical tools with the power to enhance our sexual experience profoundly. But this is not a Homegrowth to be written on a piece of paper in neatly structured steps. For, my friends, it is time to move beyond. This Homegrowth asks you to be willing to step out of day-to-day fact and into your own unique reality, a reality that will allow you to experience the growth that can lead you home.

You are entering uncharted territory. In this Homegrowth, you and your partner will create the *magic* that is yours alone. Each step in this final process I share with you—Making Love—depends upon the steps the two of you have taken previously. From now on, trust yourselves and the journey you have taken so far. Depend on each other's emotions, instincts, intellects, and imaginations to be your guides. Together, you and the one you love can finally create your own distinctive *magic*.

*Lazaris, *The Magick of Sex*, © 1981 NPN Publishing, Inc.

Let's take an in-depth look at what we can create together when we choose to genuinely make love. Don't forget each step along this journey is a special experience in itself, an experience you might never want to deprive yourself of again. When we allow the steps of this path to culminate in the *magic* of sex, we participate in the powerfully synergistic, life-changing phenomenon that is our rightful legacy.

Set and Setting

One of the first considerations in creating an authentic lovemaking experience is the set and setting. The set is the synergy of the whole lovemaking experience, while the setting refers to the actual physical location.

The set encompasses everything involved in the lovemaking experience, both tangible and intangible. This includes but is not limited to our emotions, our physicality, our combined levels of energy, our beliefs, and our willingness.

Just as we are constantly changing, the set continues to evolve with each new emotion, physical sensation, and intuition we have. Not only does the set continually change throughout the lovemaking process; it changes with each lovemaking experience.

Because the set incorporates every aspect, the setting is actually an element of the set; thus, with each alteration we make in the physical setting, the set also changes. The setting is the actual location—outside, inside, on the bed, on the floor, in the car—wherever we make love. It encompasses all the sensory enhancing paraphernalia we bring to the lovemaking experience. It is an atmosphere, an ambience created by combining particulars such as the type of bed, perfume, music, lighting, and so forth.

For example, the setting might be a candle-lit living room in the predawn hours, on a comforter of down. Or, the setting could be a fan-cooled bedroom on Sunday afternoon with music playing softly in the background, the scent of freshly cut flowers permeating the room. Whatever our desires, we can create a fresh setting to enrich each lovemaking experience.

Although I will be the first to admit that spontaneous encounters can be filled with fun and sexual satisfaction, I have given up the belief that spontaneous sex is better or more exciting than planned sex.

The fact is, many spontaneous sexual encounters are not what they have been cracked up to be. Making love on the beach usually means contending with sand, sand fleas, and other people, not to mention the weather. Cars can create very uncomfortable, even bruising situations. Hotel rooms, which can be erotic occasionally, more often than not are decorated in cold sterility. As for phone booths, well. . . . Think about it, how often has spontaneous sex really been as wonderful as the movies and books portray it?

By utilizing all of our senses to plan the intricate details of a setting, we can create an erotic, safe, comfortable, and passionate environment. However, I would also like to suggest that simply creating the atmosphere where we will share our love can be an incredibly sensual experience in itself.

For instance, by learning what scents are particularly arousing to ourselves and our lovers, we can add just the right fragrance to enliven our lovemaking. Perfumed sheets can transmit a continual subliminal message of desire.

The sense of touch or feeling can lead us to choose satin sheets instead of silk, or flannels instead of cotton. Some of us might prefer a soft feather bed, while others enjoy the floating sensation of a water bed.

Visual sensations such as color can also contribute to the quality of a sexual experience. Some colors make us feel restful and safe, while others irritate us. Colors and how we coordinate them will make all the difference in the effect.

As for sound, I find it extremely distracting to play music that has lyrics or a very familiar tune. I start humming to the music, which can be very disconcerting. Many people like music to accompany their lovemaking, however, and often choose pieces they consider to be erotic. Since this is a personal preference, both partners can decide together what music they prefer. Tapes and records with erotic sounds dubbed in under the music are also available. The sighs and sounds of people making love can be heard intermingled with the music. The sensation is similar to being in a hotel room listening to the couple next door making passionate love. For some people, this auditory experience is extremely erotic. Do you know what is erotic for you? Do you know what your partner finds erotic? If not, find out; the exploration alone could prove to be an erotic experience.

Taste is a sense that should not be neglected. Many people find the flavor of their lover's aroused body erotic, while others enhance their experience with edible lotions and creams. Still others use the kitchen as a resource for erotic pleasure, using items such as hot fudge, whipped cream, and ice cream to embellish the experience.

Remember it is important to incorporate all of our senses into our setting. When we pay attention to all of our senses and to our specific moods and emotions, we can continue to create settings that are as fresh and flowing as we would like our sexual experiences to be.

Many of us complain that sex is boring when it is too familiar. However, when we create exciting, variable settings, our lovemaking need never be boring again. Consciously change your setting; create something new and exciting as often as you wish.

Personal Foreplay

Just as the setting creates a physical atmosphere for our lovemaking, Personal Foreplay creates an atmosphere or ambience within ourselves.

When Personal Foreplay was first described to me, I remember thinking how accurately the words described the action.

Personal Foreplay is thinking about the sexual experience long before you get there or are even in contact with the other person. It is a profoundly personal experience.

I savored the most exciting lovemaking experiences with Jonathan only after I had spent the day imagining what was to come. I created an element of escalating excitement by using Personal Foreplay. I visualized the details of our time together—how he would kiss me, where and how we would disrobe. I sensed the texture of his skin, imagining myself touching him, and I heard his moans of pleasure in my mind.

I created an internal ambience, charged with sexual energy and anticipatory excitement. These kinds of sensual reflections are the essence of Personal Foreplay.

Clearly, our most potent sexual organ is our brain, for it is there we create our imaginings. In Personal Foreplay, we use our imagination to enhance our desires. The more we imagine titillating, passionate, erotic lovemaking, the more we can create it.

A Word to the Wise

As exhilarating as Personal Foreplay can be, it can also create havoc. Imagine for a moment what the outcome might be when one partner has spent the day imagining an evening filled with warm, loving passion while the other has spent the same day grappling with the stresses and dilemmas of the everyday world.

On a crisp afternoon in November, while golden leaves floated gently toward the ground, I decided the evening ahead would be perfect for making love in front of the fire. I could already hear soft music playing inside my head as I imagined Jonathan and myself lustily relishing his favorite finger foods. Oh, I spent a marvelous afternoon creating a setting to match the robust day and my passionate mood.

Needless to say, when Jonathan came home I was ready. I was dressed (or perhaps better put—not dressed) in his favorite fashion. The tantalizing aroma of freshly baked food filled the air, the fire was crackling, and the windows were opened just enough for the sounds of the evening to permeate the love nest I had created in front of the fire. Since my imagination had been working all afternoon, I could not wait to throw myself into Jonathan's arms and taste our first kiss. As he drove up, I opened the door and stood in what I hoped was an alluring pose, waiting for him to enter my sexual wonderland.

Unfortunately, I had no idea that Jonathan had spent the day driving in a traffic jam that got him to an important meeting forty minutes late and consequently diminished his ability to make the presentation he had planned. He was angry and looking forward to some alone time to think about his day and restore his equilibrium. As he approached the door, he appeared bedraggled. When he looked up and saw me, he stood stock-still, then he simply stared at the ground shaking his head. Unlike myself, he had not been thinking about sex all afternoon. He was not in a position to move his personal concerns aside to join me in lovemaking. He felt put-upon and angry. And I ended up disappointed and frustrated.

We've all experienced similar situations. Personal Foreplay is a powerful tool, but it is best used when both partners anticipate a mutual sexual experience. Personal Foreplay is a powerful aphrodisiac. However, unless both partners experience their own Personal Foreplay, they could end up angry, frustrated, and disappointed.

The Good Stuff

Foreplay is *for play*, time to play with each other, to learn about and connect with each other, to weave a spell of desire around each other and create mounting excitement. Sexual foreplay is a shared creation. During this time of physical bonding and emotional sharing, sex becomes an intimate experience we create *with* each other. It is not something we do to each other. Foreplay is a time to communicate, to connect, and to share what makes us feel good. Foreplay is the *"good stuff."*

The "good stuff" becomes intimate, connective, exciting, and erotic when both partners participate in it. We can create foreplay that is filled with laughter, passion, and sighs of desire by knowing our own bodies so well we can teach our partners what pleases us. In turn, we can learn what pleases our partners.

Foreplay is a dance. Neither partner should be dragged around the dance floor. Stepping all over your partner's feet is not necessary. Openly ask to learn the steps to your partner's dance. In turn, be willing to teach the steps to yours. Dancing in harmony with each other creates bonding. The "good stuff" helps set the stage for *magic*.

Intercourse and Orgasm

Intercourse is the physical union. It can also be the communion created between ourselves and our partners. Orgasm is the physical and emotional release of all the energy thus far created between ourselves and our partners. It can also be an immense merging of energies. When we are willing to move past the physical union as we have all experienced it, and explore the communion that is possible, we can gain a better understanding of the enormous impact of intercourse.

Communion is one of the optimum outcomes of intercourse. Combining the physical union with a profound level of emotional communication creates a bond or communion that elevates intercourse to a new level of intimacy. When we are as close as physically possible, we can become bonded in ways we can feel but may not see. Our electromagnetic fields can merge with those of our lovers, allowing us to break down many of our emotional barriers. This type of emotional communication creates a level of vulnerability available at few other times.

When we combine the physical union of intercourse with

this emotional communication, we can allow our emotions to flow freely with no obstructions. This intensity of communicating with our emotions enhances our tenderness, trust, compassion, and love. Intercourse that embraces this heartfelt communion as well as the physical union allows us to drop as many barriers as we dare. In uniting with another being, we create an opportunity to be more than we previously were. Most of us think of orgasm as an intense physical pleasure, but it is much more. Orgasm is a magical dance between our cells and our souls. When they are so filled with energy, they explode into a rhapsody of pleasure. But orgasm is more than this dance, more than a release. It is a re-creation.

During the orgasmic explosion, an immense charge of energy radiates through our beings, possibly affecting every one of our cells. When the charge passes, our cells settle down again, regrouping with the surrounding cells. This regrouping combined with the amount of energy each cell chooses to hold, can differ from the state of the cell before orgasm. This is one way orgasm allows us the opportunity to re-create ourselves.

If we desire, we can use orgasm's massive amount of energy to heal our emotional distress, to enhance and bond our love, and to increase and enlighten our life's joy. Like the first sunburst of a new day, lighting the beauty of the earth, orgasm can light the beauty within ourselves.

Creating this optimum experience will be enough for many of us. At this point, we can, if we choose, be different than we were before, ending the experience here by having a communion with our partners that bonds us in a way that enriches our lives with intimacy and joy.

For others of us, however, the search for the *magic* will compel us to move beyond. . . .

Beyond All Time and Space

As we move into the realms of sexual *magic*, we go beyond our concept of linear time. We can begin to understand the *magic* by moving out of our traditional perception of time and delving into that dimension between time and space.

The following two steps toward creating *magic* take place in that little-known, less-understood dimension. So intricately interwoven, they defy description in everyday terms. Yet, we will benefit from attempting to understand them because, together, these two steps create that inexplicable fusion— the *magic* of sex.

Mental Orgasm

We can experience the phenomenon of mental orgasm when we allow that re-creation we spoke of above to transpire in every fiber of our being. This means not only in our physical cells as in intercourse and orgasm, but also in our emotional and spiritual beings as well. The energy associated with mental orgasm is so vast, it has the capacity to consume us totally.

Mental orgasm is the resurrection or re-creation of ourselves. It destroys all that we are. Then, in the next instant, it recreates us anew. The French refer to this experience as the "little death." However, the experience goes beyond death, for death always brings rebirth. When we experience mental orgasm, no part of us is left untouched or unchanged. We are truly reborn!

With the participation of our entire being, we prepare ourselves to move beyond who we are into the magic of what we can be. Essentially, mental orgasm opens the doors that allow us to take the next step into the unknown.

As we have stated before, each step in this journey toward *magic* is inherently important. Although this technically holds true for these two steps, it is highly improbable that we would stop this immense momentum of energy and not continue to create the *magic* in Personal Release.

Personal Release

During mental orgasm—at that micromoment between death and rebirth—we shift into the dimension between space and time. In this dimension, being as vulnerable as humanly possible, we have the rare opportunity "to touch the face of God." Personal Release is the ultimate vulnerability, the ultimate letting go, the ultimate power.

When we experience mental orgasm in unison with our partner, we open the doors to our souls. The light that is the core of our beingness soars out of our bodies, into that unfathomable realm beyond all space and time, to touch with a spark of God/Goddess/All That Is. Miraculously, by touching with the love that is God/Goddess/All That Is, we are changed forever; this is Personal Release.

The changes that occur during Personal Release may manifest themselves in various ways. When we touch with total love, we can allow ourselves to be healed of our emotional, physical, or spiritual wounds. We can allow all our positive attributes to be enhanced by love. This love can enable us to let go of our emotional blockages, our childhood hurts, and our nonproductive beliefs. Love becomes a part of us when we allow ourselves to touch the All That Is.

This is the part of sex that changes us, this is fusion, the creation of something more that leads us to the new set and setting. This is the *magic*. This is what the journey has been about.

New Set and Setting

Life is an ongoing circle. We end where we begin and will once again begin where we end. We started lovemaking by creating a set and setting that would best enhance our personal experience. Now we have come full circle, ending at the point we began, the set and setting.

When we create sex to be more than just a physical experience, when we are changed by the love of the All That Is, we are reborn and thus experience ourselves and everything around us in a new way.

After Personal Release, when we settle back into our bodies, everything around us will be different. Our lover will be new, too. We will experience the room and the ambience we have created from the perspective of the new people we have become during our lovemaking. The next time we make love, we will begin from this place of newness. Since we are always changing, we will always create something new.

For me, the search for the *magic* has finally come to fruition. Nothing will ever be the same again.

Epilogue

Since I began to write this book, the years have flown swiftly, while I have continued to change and evolve. Jonathan and I ended our relationship years ago. But the learning that I did while with him continues to serve me. Sometimes, I am amazed at the quantity and quality of *magic* and love I create in my life by utilizing the same processes I have shared with you thoughout this book.

My search for myself has never ended; it continues to grow and stretch, taking me to places I never dreamed possible. My journey is no longer frantic, and I find that I use fear and anger less often to motivate myself. I search because it is fun, because I am curious, but most of all, because there is an inexplicable drive in me to do so.

Today my focus is on my spirituality, on creating a deeper, more authentic relationship with God/Goddess/All That Is. Once again I have turned inward to find the questions that lead me closer to me. I am currently developing a more loving and meaningful relationship with my Higher Consciousness. In more and more ways, I understand that I do create my own reality—all of it.

Thank you for allowing me to share my journey with you, and for sharing yours with me. Remember that within you is everything you will ever need; treat yourself with gentleness and kindness each and every day of your life.

Meditation Appendix

Self-Exploration Through Meditation/Visualization

Welcome to the realm of meditation. Welcome to an ancient wonder—self-exploration through guided visualization. The following meditations are specifically designed to complete the UnlimitedGrowth process outlined in Chapter Two. Recording the two carefully structured meditations in your own voice will allow you to guide your own meditation. Or, if you wish, you may purchase an audiotape of the same meditations guided by Kimberley Heart. Simply complete the convenient order form in the back of the book.

Creating Your Safe Place

In order to begin your journey inward, it is important to feel safe and secure. A safe environment encourages your willingness to explore the intricacies of your unknown self. Before you begin either meditation, you will want to create a safe place in your imagination.

After you have relaxed your body and mind, imagine yourself out in nature; you can use an actual setting or one that exists purely in your imagination. For instance, you might find yourself in the heart of a forest, on the dunes of a sandy beach, or in a spring garden.

Exploring all your senses, notice what you want to see, touch, smell, hear, and feel while you are in your safe place. Remember to use color, texture, and sound to help you create whatever is right for you. You might imagine lilies floating serenely on a still pond. Or you might prefer waves that crash upon the rocks reflecting riotous colors in the sunlight. You can create gusting winds that tear at your clothing or gentle breezes that softly ruffle your hair.

Creating a place of safety is a flexible and changing process. With each meditation, you can expand, delete, or begin anew. There is only one requisite for your safe place: A camp fire will always be burning brightly, a beacon to guide you home.

Spend as much time as you need to create your safe place. Trust yourself to create whatever you need to feel safe, relaxed, and at peace. When you are comfortable in your safe place, you may begin these meditations.

Meditation 1: Finally Free

→ Establish your safe place as described above.

→ Choose a time and a place where you can feel safe, relaxed, and not be interrupted.

→ Sit in a comfortable position. Relax. Use any form of relaxation that works for you. There is no one right way, just a way that works best for you. Take as much, or as little, time as necessary.

[For example, to help you relax, you might surround yourself in a bubble of golden light. Breathing in the relaxation, allow your body to relax with each exhalation. Or you might like to focus on different body parts. Beginning at your toes and working up to your head, allow each part to let go and relax. If you prefer, use a yoga breathing technique, if you know one. Perhaps you are most successful just allowing

yourself to drift, as if you were daydreaming. Explore and discover a form of relaxation that works best for you.]

[*Begin recording here.*]

Once you are relaxed, begin to count yourself into an ever deeper state of relaxation by counting backward from twelve to one. Count slowly, and with each number ask yourself to go deeper and deeper into a state of relaxation and peace.

When you reach the number one, find yourself in your safe place. Allow your senses to awaken one at a time. With your mind's eye, begin to visualize the details of your safe place. Envision the colors of the trees and the sky, the various hues of the camp fire. Feel the soft lick of a blade of grass as you lightly run your palm across it, or sense the tug of sand under your feet as the waves kiss your toes before returning to the sea. Whatever your safe place is like, allow it to gather around you. Sit, lie, or stand in your safe place; just "be" for a short while. Allow safety to change you. Allow safety to prepare you.

Moving to the edge of safety, make a decision to move into the unknown, to explore self-forgiveness. Step across the threshold of safety into a wonderful forest.

Notice the different sizes of the trees—some ancient and powerful, some newly born with lime green sprouts reaching for the sun. As you walk deeper into the forest, notice the shadows of the trees upon the ground. Step over the fallen limbs and around rocks and boulders that might be in your way. How does it feel to walk upon the forest floor? Every now and then, a tree seems to reach out and gently touch you with its leaves. Listen to the sounds of the vibrant, living forest. Allow all your senses to be involved. Feel alive; taste, listen, touch.

Quicken your pace, walking deeper into the unknown. Search now for a way into the earth herself. Perhaps you will find a hollowed-out tree with a spiral staircase to take you down, down into the earth. Perhaps you will stumble upon an ancient tree stump. If you look very closely, you may find an opening that reveals a path leading down, down into the heart of the earth. Or perhaps you will come to the opening of a cave that is slightly hidden. At the back of this cave, there is an entrance leading into the earth. Discover your opening and begin to travel down, down, into the earth.

[*Seeing is only one sense; remember to continue using all of your senses. The more excitement and aliveness you put into the visualization, the more impactful and lasting the changes.*]

Find a torch stuck into the wall and light it. Lighting your own way into the earth, travel deeper and deeper, feeling the moistness, smelling the fresh scent. At times, you step tenuously, letting your toes tell your heels when to touch down. At other times, find yourself moving rapidly down wide caverns, almost running with excitement in your exploration. Cross underground streams and traverse caverns so deep and wide you can't begin to see across their width. Travel through corridors of stalactites, reaching up to touch them. Keep moving down, exploring farther and farther into the earth, searching.

[*As you enter the following caves, give yourself enough time in each to experience the full range of feelings that come up for you.*]

Searching for the cave of forgiveness, allow your curiosity to lead you. Listen for the cave calling to you. As you step around a bend, a flash of light reflected from your torch—ruby red light—catches your eye. Holding your torch higher, your heart beats faster as you move swiftly toward your discovery. Reach out to touch what the light seems to be embracing, reflecting. Feel the inviting warmth of a cluster of rubies. Follow the trail of rubies to their cave, a cave you would have missed if they had not shown you the way.

Peer into the cave engulfed in the astounding brilliance of red. Finally remembering to move your feet, step into the cave itself. When you lift the torch high above your head, the rubies magnify the light until it seems to have a life of its own. The entire cave is illuminated and radiates red. Red surrounds you and is absorbed by you. Breathe in red and see only red. Red is everywhere you turn. The power and security of red is a part of you.

Search this cave for three rubies that are meant for you. Some may call to your mind, saying, "Take me, take me." Your special rubies might vibrate when you touch them, or perhaps they make your heart sing. Find the three gems that are just right for you.

After you have found your gems, notice the light toward the back of the cave. It seems to take on a different hue. Move toward the changing light. Stooping as you make your way through the passageway you discover, emerge into a second cave. Straightening your body, you are awe struck. The light in here changes to riotous orange. Poppy orange springs at you, reflected from the orange topaz that lines the walls of this cave. The orange makes you laugh with pleasure. Orange is everywhere; breathe it in, allowing it to permeate every inch of you.

When you are ready, as you did with the rubies, select three topaz crystals that are just right for you.

Your feet lead you through another passage. Excited and curious at the prospect of what might be next, you wonder if anything can surpass what you have already experienced.

As your journey takes you into another cave, it appears as if you have walked into the heart of the sun. Buttery yellow greets you, sings to you, and surrounds you. There is so much yellow in this cave, you seem to be yellow, seeing and breathing only yellow. Once you adjust to the yellow splendor, notice the gems that create such magic—yellow sapphires. Perhaps feelings pour through you. Allow them.

When you are ready, find the three yellow sapphires meant for you. Still vibrating with yellow, move along the passage to the next cave.

As you walk, a stillness reaches out to you, a gentleness so delicate it emanates power. As you step into the cave of emeralds, green floats to you and embraces you. Take in the emerald green with your eyes, through your heart, and with your lungs. Allow the gentle wonder of the vibrant green emeralds to touch you, to love you. Feel.

Stay in the quiet power of the emeralds. When you are ready, select the three emeralds meant expressly for you.

Next move into the cave of blue sapphires. The blue takes your breath away. Holding your torch high, take in the blue that is everywhere. Spinning around and around, listen to the blue as it speaks to you. It is as if the magnificent sapphires want to commune with you. When you are ready, find your three special sapphires.

Journeying into the cave of amethysts is like entering a giant geode. Indigo—royal purple—leaps out majestically to surround you. Reach out; touch the indigo in the air. Breathe in and marvel at its wonder. Take as much time as you need. When you are ready, this time choose *four* gems, adding them to your riches.

As you continue to explore, discover a small rounded cave. As you step in, a brilliant white light blinds you. As your senses adjust, notice that this precious cave is filled with diamonds. These diamonds are infinitely pure, each with a heart of lavender. As you breathe in the white-violet light, the top of your head seems to expand. Feeling the grace of these diamonds, your eyes glimmer with tears. When you are ready, reach down and take a handful.

As you blink away your tears, another corridor catches your eye. Attracted by the light glowing at its end, you think the diamonds are continuing their reflection. But this light has a different hue. Follow the light and step out of the corridor into a beautiful sunny day. Here, deep in the earth, the sun shines and the grass grows.

With your arms and hands filled, look for a place to put your precious gems. Not faraway, you see the still, quiet Pool of True Reflections. Next to the pool is a large boulder. Place your gems—your gifts—on the flat surface of the boulder. Arrange your gems in a way that makes you smile. These gems are offerings. You have brought them to the altar of forgiveness by the Pool of True Reflections.

The pool, so deep, so richly beautiful, reflects the truth of all that gaze into it. Somehow you know you will see your reflection in the magical pool. This is not the reflection you see in your everyday mirror; it is the reflection of the part of you that you have come to forgive—the ugly you.

[*You have prepared yourself for this. You have discovered your uglies. You no longer kid yourself. You know you can be, and have been hurtful to others. That is why you are here, to forgive the why of your ugliness. Or perhaps you are ready now to forgive more than the whys. Perhaps you are ready to forgive the actions themselves—the whats.*]

Step up to the Pool of True Reflections. Allowing yourself to feel, take a deep breath and look into the pool.

The first sight of your ugliness startles you. Look at those eyes gazing back at you. You didn't expect to see such anger . . . pain . . . self-pity . . . guilt. But look into those eyes that stare back at you. They don't lie. See how warped this part of you—the part that is capable of great ugliness—has become. Don't turn away. *Look. See. Feel.* Oh, you would like to believe the only person this ugly part of you has hurt was yourself. But you have become more honest than that. You know you have hurt others. You see it in the eyes staring back at you. You see it in the grimace around the mouth, in the shadows around the eyes. They all tell the truth. Look, look at this part of you. Look at the ugliness of you.

Remember *why* you did what you did.

Oh, yes, now you remember, and as you remember, begin to feel compassion for this ugly you.

As you adjust your head to see your ugliness from all angles, notice that the reflection in the pond does not move with you. Then, to your amazement, the ugly you steps back. Whirling around, you see, standing several steps in front of you, the ugly you! It had been breathing over your shoulder most of your life, but you refused to notice. Do not turn away. Do not run.

Remember.

Remember how and why you became so ugly. Remember and focus on the *why.* Remember you can forgive yourself only by facing this part of you. Your heart opens to this ugly you. Feel compassion and forgiveness for this bent, deformed, and distorted you.

As your heart opens and forgiveness reigns, glance at your offering. The sun has caught the light of the gems, creating a rainbow that arcs over your head and down upon the head of the ugly you.

As you open your heart to forgiveness, the rainbow changes to an arc of purple light. Look at this ugly you and say, "I forgive you." With all your heart and mind, say it two more times, "I forgive you. I forgive you." From head to toe, the ugly you stands in a shaft of purple light. Before your marveling eyes, the ugly you is transformed into a radiant being surrounded in purple light.

Open your arms and step toward the light. Step into the purple light and hold this forgiven you. Hold it tighter and tighter until, as you inhale deeply, it merges into you and becomes one with you.

Now, it is you standing in the purple light, holding onto yourself. Taste the tears of joy and gratitude upon your lips. Hold yourself, hold the forgiven you. Feel.

When you are ready, bring yourself out of meditation by counting up from one to five. Or use any other method that works for you.

Meditation 2: Changing Your Beliefs

Each of us is unique in our desires and preferences. The following meditation offers three distinct options. Select the one that best fits your personality and your comfort zone.

Follow the detailed instructions described in Meditation 1:

→ Relax and go into meditation.
→ Go to your safe place.
→ Move to the edge of safety and step into the unknown.
→ Travel through the unknown and find your way into the earth.
→ Travel down into the earth, into the inner world of your subconscious.

[*Begin recording here.*]

Remembering to use all your senses, travel down into the inner world. Begin looking for a corridor. It might be a corridor burrowed out of solid rock with a rounded ceiling and roughened walls. Or perhaps it is a simple corridor typical of any building. find the corridor in your inner world and step into it.

As you walk along the corridor, you will find three doors. Each door is clearly marked. The first door is labeled Hall of Records; the second reads Computer Room; and the final door is called the Ancient Room of Scrolls. Choose one, remembering there is no right or wrong selection—just one that is most comfortable for you.

Select one door. Examine its shape, texture, and latch. Placing your hand on the latch, open the door just enough to step inside. Close the door softly behind you.

Hall of Records

As you step through the doorway, look around and notice. You might be in a massive building with stately columns and fifty-foot ceilings. Perhaps your Hall of Records is a small wood building, like a town hall. Let your imagination work. Let it help you see what is there for you.

If you are outside the building, go in.

Find the information desk, fill out the card the attendant hands you. In the space marked, "Information Desired," write, "Record of Beliefs." Next, write the exact belief you have come to change. Give the card to the attendant who looks up the file number.

When your file card is returned to you, the file number is written on it. Follow the attendant's directions to the correct file cabinet.

You might travel down long halls with marble floors, up grand staircases, and through multiple rooms in search of the file cabinet where this belief is stored. Or you might simply need to cross to the far side of the room.

Whatever is true for you, find the correct file cabinet.

Once you have located the correct file cabinet, match the number clearly printed on the front of the cabinet with the number on your card. Finding the correct drawer, open it. Feel the weight of the drawer as you pull it open; listen to the sound it makes. As your fingers move over the top of each individual file, read the printed numbers until you find the file you are looking for. Once you find it, push the others slightly back, tugging this one out of the drawer. Place the card in the drawer to mark the file's place.

Take your file to a private table and open it. On a clean sheet of paper, written in your distinctive script, is the belief you have come to change.

As you read this old belief one last time, feel your feelings.

Feel your determination to end the belief. This is why you have journeyed here—to change this belief. You understand your pay-offs. You have forgiven yourself. Now it is time to end this old belief and replace it with a new, more productive belief.

Stay focused, stay determined, stay committed as you destroy this belief in three different ways.

First, pick up the pen you find lying on the table next to the marble ash tray. Write "VOID" in bold, determined strokes across your belief. With each stroke of the pen, your determination and feelings tell your subconscious mind to delete this belief from its memory; you are telling your subconscious mind to change.

With the last stroke of your pen, underline the word "VOID" vehemently.

Pick up the single sheet of paper. Fold it in half, then in half again. With each fold, focus on the fact that you are ending this belief forever.

Now as you *rip* the folded page into tiny pieces, feel your determination and commitment with each rip.

Now pick up the matchbook lying in the marble ashtray and light one match.

Light one scrap of the torn paper and drop it into the ashtray. Feeding the other scraps into the fire, watch the hungry flames consume every bit of your old belief. Watch the flames turn the paper from yellow to red to black and finally to gray. When you are certain every scrap is burned and extinguished, dump the ashes into the trash bin under the table.

Return your attention to the open file folder, where you find a clean sheet of paper. Write your new belief in a clear, bold hand. Make each letter deliberate and determined. As you write, feel what your life will be like with this new belief. Hold that resonance as you write.

Read your new belief again, feeling the magnitude of what you have done.

Close the file and return it to the file cabinet. Remove the card you placed there, returning the file to the exact place you found it. Feel. Hold the resonance.

Quietly, with respect, leave the Hall of Records. Open the door just enough to easily slide through, then close it gently behind you. Lean against the door for a moment, allowing yourself to feel the excitement and to celebrate what you have accomplished.

Quickly find your way back through the corridor and up, up and out of the inner world, through the place you entered. Move back into your safe place.

Celebrate, dance, shout with delight. Imagine how your life will be different. Visualize how your life will be now. Hold the resonance. Let it be done. Allow it to be real.

Computer Room

As you step into the computer room, look around and notice. You may be alone in a small white room with only a few pieces of equipment, or you may be in a large room with other people and many computer terminals. Let your imagination help you see what is there for you.

Walk to a computer terminal and pull out the comfortable chair. As you relax in the chair, turn the computer on. The computer prints "Welcome" across the screen. Type, "Access Beliefs" and press "Return." "What beliefs?" the computer asks. Enter the belief you wish to change. "Please wait," the computer asks as it scans its memory. Wait until the computer flashes "Found" on the screen. When it does, press "Return" twice. The belief you have come to change is printed on the screen.

As you read this old belief one last time, feel your feelings.

Feel your determination to end the belief. This is why you have come here—to change this belief. You understand your payoffs. You have forgiven yourself. Now it is time to end this old belief and replace it with a new, more productive belief.

Stay focused, stay determined, stay committed as you destroy this belief in three different ways.

First, using the electronic pen attached by a thin cable to the computer, write the word "VOID" on the computer slate located to the right of your terminal. The slate transfers anything you write on it to the computer screen.

Watch the handwriting appear across the computer screen.

With each stroke of the pen, your determination and feelings tell your subconscious mind to delete this belief from its memory; you are telling your subconscious mind to change. With the last stroke of your pen, underline the word "VOID" vehemently.

Press the "Delete" key. When the computer asks, "Are you sure? (Y/N)," press the "Y" key with finality. Immediately, both the computer screen and slate becomes blank. Automatically erasing the belief from all its memory banks, the computer makes a single copy on a floppy disk and ejects it.

Remove the disk from the computer and take it to the electronic shredder. Turn the shredder on, listening to the low hum of its motor. Watch its razor teeth waiting to destroy anything it is fed.

Realizing that you are ending the belief forever, push it through the teeth of the shredder. Feel your feelings.

Take the shredded fragments and throw them into the fireproof trash can. Next, ignite the fragments with a lighted match. Watch the tiny explosions as each piece of metal oxide film turns red, then blue, and finally vaporizes. When nothing is left but a bit of ash, replace the lid on the trash can.

Using the electronic pen, write your new belief on the slate. Make each stroke clear and concise. Keep your focus and determination. Feel what life will be like now that you have this new belief. Read the new belief written on the computer screen.

Press "Save." Listen to the familiar bleep and groans of your computer as it saves this belief safely in its memory. It cannot be lost or accidentally erased.

Read your new belief and feel the magnitude of what you have done. Hold the resonance.

Turn off the computer.

Quietly, with respect, leave the Computer Room. Open the door just enough to easily slide through and close it gently behind you. Lean against the door for a moment, allowing yourself to feel the excitement and to celebrate what you have accomplished.

Quickly find your way back through the corridor and up, up and out of the inner world, through the place you entered. Move back into your safe place.

Celebrate, dance, shout with delight. Imagine how your life will be now. Visualize how your life will be different. Hold the resonance. Let it be done. Allow it to be real.

Ancient Room of Scrolls

As you step into the room of scrolls, take a moment to look around. You might find yourself in a templelike room, its walls lined with scroll holders. Each holder is identified by shelf letter and scroll number. Or your room might be in an ancient cave with scrolls stored in the same manner. Whatever your room looks like, let your imagination work. Let your imagination help you see what is there for you.

Silently walk to the scroll table. Small padded clips used to hold the unrolled scrolls gently in place are attached to the table. Next to the clips is a copper bowl. A lighted votive candle is cleverly mounted on the side of the copper bowl. Next to the bowl is a quill pen, ink, and an ancient ink blotter.

Notice an old piece of parchment attached to one of the clips. Gently remove it. Written on this piece of parchment is a shelf letter and scroll number. The paper might read "Shelf G, Scroll 14."

The shelf letter and scroll number is the location of the belief you have come to change. Taking the scrap of parchment with you, find the shelf you are looking for.

Carefully take the scroll from its place and walk back to the scroll table. Remove the string, or slide off the scroll ring. Unroll the scroll and read the belief you have come to change.

As you read this old belief one last time, feel your feelings. Feel your determination to end the belief. This is why you have journeyed here—to change this belief. You understand your payoffs. You have forgiven yourself. Now it is time to end this old belief and replace it with a new, more productive belief.

Stay focused, stay determined, and stay committed as you destroy this belief in three different ways.

First, using the quill pen, write "VOID" across the belief you have come to change.

With each stroke of the pen, your determination and feelings tell your subconscious mind to delete this belief from its memory; you are telling your subconscious mind to change. With the last stroke of your pen, underline the word "VOID" vehemently.

Pick up the scroll and fold it in half, then in half again. With each fold, focus on the fact that you are ending this belief forever.

Now *rip* the scroll into tiny pieces. Feel your determination and commitment with each rip.

Now, with the flame from the votive candle, carefully light one scrap of the torn parchment and drop it into the copper bowl. Feed each piece into the flame. Stay focused on the fact that you are destroying this belief. Feel your determination to be done with this belief. Watch the hungry flames consume each bit of the old belief. The flames turn the fragments of scroll from yellow to red to black and finally to gray. When you are certain every scrap is burned and extinguished, dump the ashes into the bin under the scroll table.

Find a clean sheet of parchment waiting for you. Using the quill pen, write your new belief with even, bold strokes. Concentrate on each movement of the pen. How does it feel to have this new belief be a part of your life?

Seal each word into the parchment with the blotter.

Read your new belief and feel the magnitude of what you have done. Hold the resonance.

Gently roll the scroll and tie it or slip the scroll ring around it. Return the scroll to the same location you found the other scroll.

Quietly, with respect, leave the Ancient Room of Scrolls. Open the door just enough to easily slide through and close it gently behind you. Lean against the door for a moment, allowing yourself to feel the excitement and to celebrate what you have accomplished.

Quickly find your way back through the corridor and up and out of the inner world, through the place you entered. Move back into your safe place.

Celebrate, dance, shout with delight. Imagine how your life will be different. Visualize the picture of your life now. Hold the resonance. Let it be done. Allow it to be real.

Permissions

The author wishes to express her thanks and appreciation to those who granted permission to use the following material:

Michael Benner for permission to quote from *Easy Alpha*, audio tape, copyright © 1986 by Michael Benner. Used by permission of Michael Benner.

Little, Brown and Company for permission to quote from *The Undiscovered Self* by Carl Jung. Reprinted by permission.

Lucinda McDermott, Ph.D., for permission to quote from "Au Courant Glossary," copyright © 1968 by Forerunner Publications. Reprinted by permission of Lucinda McDermott.

NPN Publishing, Inc. for permission to use the Lazaris Material, copyright ©NPN Publishing, Inc. Used by permission.

Random House, Inc., for permission to quote from *The Book* by Alan Watts, copyright © 1966 Random House, Inc. Reprinted by permission.

St. Martin's Press for permission to use Albert Einstein quotation from *The Global Brain* by Peter Russell, copyright © 1983 J. P. Tarcher. Reprinted by permission of St. Martin's Press.

Gunther Stuhlmann for permission to quote from *A Woman Speaks: The Lectures, Seminars, and Interviews of Anaïs Nin*. Edited by Evelyn J. Hinz. Copyright © 1975 by Anaïs Nin. All rights reserved. Reprinted by permission of the Author's Representative, Gunther Stuhlmann.

Bibliography

Index to Categories

To help you locate resources that address the issues that most interest you, I have broken this Bibliography into categories. The following list will give you an overview.

Meditations, Tapes, and Booklets

The Unlimited Tapes can be obtained by calling or writing:

Kimberley Heart Unlimited
6000 Woodman Avenue, Suite A/Dept. S
Van Nuys, CA 91401
Phone: (818) 781-4769

Family Issues

Heart, Kimberley. *Introducing the Child-Self*. Van Nuys, CA: Unlimited, 1991.

Spirituality

Heart, Kimberley. *Introducing the Old Man*. Van Nuys, CA: Unlimited, 1991.

Heart, Kimberley. *Introducing the Anima*. Van Nuys, CA: Unlimited, 1991.

Lazaris Tapes

The Lazaris Material can be purchased by calling or writing:

NPN Publishing, Inc.
302 South County Road, Suite 109
Palm Beach, FL 33480
Phone: (407) 588-9599

The Lazaris Material may also be purchased by contacting Kimberley Heart Unlimited as listed above.

Lecture and Meditation

The following audio tapes offer both discussion and meditation.

Deeper Understanding

Lazaris. *Reality Creation: The Basics*. Palm Beach, FL: NPN Publishing, Inc., 1990.

Healing Abuse

Lazaris. *Ending Self-Punishment*. Palm Beach, FL: NPN Publishing, Inc., 1986.

Lazaris. *Healing and Releasing Hurt: The Keys to Happiness.* Palm Beach, FL: NPN Publishing, Inc., 1986.

Lazaris. *Ending the Pain.* Palm Beach, FL: NPN Publishing, Inc., 1988.

Lazaris. *I Deserve.* Palm Beach, FL: NPN Publishing, Inc., 1988.

Lazaris. *Ending Shame.* Palm Beach, FL: NPN Publishing, Inc., 1990.

Lazaris. *Ending Shame II: Breaking Your Psychic Contracts of Pain.* Palm Beach, FL: NPN Publishing, Inc., 1990.

Lazaris. *Stop Feeling Not Good Enough.* Palm Beach, FL: NPN Publishing, Inc., 1990.

Lazaris. *Ending Shame III: The Adolescent Years.* Palm Beach, FL: NPN Publishing, Inc., 1991.

Lazaris. *Ending Shame IV: The Adult Years.* Palm Beach, FL: NPN Publishing, Inc., 1991.

Life Issues

FEELINGS

Lazaris. *The Synergy of Trust.* Palm Beach, FL: NPN Publishing, Inc., 1981.

Lazaris. *Happiness.* Palm Beach, FL: NPN Publishing, Inc., 1984.

Lazaris. *On Releasing Guilt/On Receiving Love.* Palm Beach, FL: NPN Publishing, Inc., 1984.

Lazaris. *Ending Loneliness.* Palm Beach, FL: NPN Publishing, Inc., 1986.

Lazaris. *Fear: The Internal War.* Palm Beach, FL: NPN Publishing, Inc., 1986.

Lazaris. *Forgiving Yourself.* Palm Beach, FL: NPN Publishing, Inc., 1986.

Lazaris. *On Releasing Anger/On Releasing Self-Pity.* Palm Beach, FL: NPN Publishing, Inc., 1986.

Love

Lazaris. *Being Loved.* Palm Beach, FL: NPN Publishing, Inc., 1985.

Lazaris. *Loving.* Palm Beach, FL: NPN Publishing, Inc., 1986.

Meditations

Lazaris. *Getting More Magic Out of Your Meditations.* Palm Beach, FL: NPN Publishing, Inc., 1990.

Lazaris. *Enhancing Visualization.* Palm Beach, FL: NPN Publishing, Inc., 1991.

Relationships

Lazaris. *Intimacy.* Palm Beach, FL: NPN Publishing, Inc., 1986.

Lazaris. *The Magic of Relationships.* Palm Beach, FL: NPN Publishing, Inc., 1986.

Lazaris. *Creating, Building and Keeping Intimate Relationships.* Palm Beach, FL: NPN Publishing, Inc., 1991.

Self-Growth

Lazaris. *The Crisis of Martyrhood.* Palm Beach, FL: NPN Publishing, Inc., 1984.

Lazaris. *Self-Confidence.* Palm Beach, FL: NPN Publishing, Inc., 1984.

Lazaris. *Ending Self-Punishment.* Palm Beach, FL: NPN Publishing, Inc., 1986.

Lazaris. *Self-Esteem.* Palm Beach, FL: NPN Publishing, Inc., 1986.

Lazaris. *Self-Worth/Self-Respect.* Palm Beach, FL: NPN Publishing, Inc., 1986.

Lazaris. *Ending Self-Sabotage.* Palm Beach, FL: NPN Publishing, Inc., 1987.

Spirituality

Lazaris. *The Goddess Series, Part I.* Palm Beach, FL: NPN Publishing, Inc., 1985.

Lazaris. *The Goddess Series, Part II*. Palm Beach, FL: NPN Publishing, Inc., 1986.

Lazaris. *The Secrets of Spirituality I*. Palm Beach, FL: NPN Publishing, Inc., 1986.

Lazaris. *The Secrets of Spirituality II*. Palm Beach, FL: NPN Publishing, Inc., 1986.

Success

Lazaris. *The Power of Dominion*. Palm Beach, FL: NPN Publishing, Inc., 1984.

Lazaris. *Consciously Creating Success*. Palm Beach, FL: NPN Publishing, Inc., 1986.

Lazaris. *Excellence*. Palm Beach, FL: NPN Publishing, Inc., 1986.

Lazaris. *Unlocking the Power of Changing Your Life*. Palm Beach, FL: NPN Publishing, Inc., 1986.

Lazaris. *Abundance: The Skill*. Palm Beach, FL: NPN Publishing, Inc., 1987.

Lazaris. *New Dynamics of Processing and Programming*. Palm Beach, FL: NPN Publishing, Inc., 1989.

Meditation Only

The following audio tapes contain meditations only.

Health and Healing

Lazaris. *Handling Menstruation*. Palm Beach, FL: NPN Publishing, Inc., 1986.

Life Issues

FEELINGS

Lazaris. *Reducing Fear and Worry/Reducing Stress*. Palm Beach, FL: NPN Publishing, Inc., 1984.

Lazaris. *Handling Depression/Loneliness*. Palm Beach, FL: NPN Publishing, Inc., 1989.

Lazaris. *Happiness/Peace.* Palm Beach, FL: NPN Publishing, Inc., 1989.

Love

Lazaris. *Love/Self-Love.* Palm Beach, FL: NPN Publishing, Inc., 1989.

Success

Lazaris. *Personal Power/Power and Dominion.* Palm Beach, FL: NPN Publishing, Inc., 1984.
Lazaris. *Productivity/Impeccability.* Palm Beach, FL: NPN Publishing, Inc., 1984.
Lazaris. *Self-Confidence/Self-Awareness.* Palm Beach, FL: NPN Publishing, Inc., 1984.

Books

Between the Lines

Bach, Richard. *Illusions.* New York: Dell, 1977.
Bradley, Marion. *The Mists of Avalon.* New York: Ballantine, 1982.
Paulus, Trina. *Hope for the Flowers.* New York: Paulist Press, 1972.
Saint-Exupery, Antoine de. *The Little Prince.* New York: Harcourt, Brace and World, 1943.

Deeper Understandings

Hawking, Stephen. *A Brief History of Time.* New York: Bantam, 1988.
Hoff, Benjamin. *The Tao of Pooh.* New York: Dutton, 1983.
Silverstein, Shel. *The Giving Tree.* New York: Harper and Row, 1964.

Family Issues

Bradshaw, John. *Bradshaw on: The Family.* Deerfield Beach, FL: Health Communications, 1988.

Leman, Kevin. *The Birth Order.* New York: Dell, 1985.

Satir, Virginia. *Peoplemaking.* Palo Alto, CA: Science and Behavior Books, 1972.

CHILDREN

Briggs, Dorothy. *Your Child's Self-Esteem.* New York: Doubleday, 1970.

Kraizer, Sherryll. *The Safe Child Book.* New York: Dell, 1985.

Van der Zande, Irene. *1, 2, 3 . . . The Toddler Years.* Santa Cruz, CA: Toddler Care Center, 1986.

FAMILY RELATIONSHIPS

Bloomfield, Harold. *Making Peace With Your Parents.* New York: Ballantine, 1983.

Forward, Susan. *Toxic Parents.* New York: Bantam, 1989.

Friday, Nancy. *My Mother/My Self: The Daughter's Search for Identity.* New York: Dell, 1977.

Leonard, Linda Schierse. *The Wounded Woman: Healing the Father-Daughter Relationship.* Boston: Shambhala, 1982.

Healing Abuse

Bass, Ellen, and Laura Davis. *The Courage to Heal: A Guide for Women Survivors of Child Sexual Abuse.* New York: Perennial Library, Harper and Row, 1988.

Bradshaw, John. *Healing the Shame That Binds You.* Deerfield Beach, FL: Health Communications, 1988.

Lew. *Victims No Longer.* New York: HarperCollins, 1990. (For male victims of sexual abuse.)

Health and Healing

Boston Women's Health Collective. *The New Our Bodies, Ourselves: A Book by and for Women.* New York: Simon and Schuster, 1984.

Hay, Louise. *You Can Heal Your Life*. Santa Monica, CA: Hay House, 1988.

Hay, Louise. *Love Your Body*. Santa Monica, CA: Hay House 1989.

Hufnagel, Vicki. *No More Hysterectomies*. New York: Penguin, 1989.

Siegel, Bernie. *Love, Medicine and Miracles*. New York: Harper and Row, 1989.

Siegel, Bernie. *Peace, Love and Healing*. New York: Harper and Row, 1989.

Life Issues

Viscott, David. *Risking*. New York: Pocket Books, 1976.

Love

Buscaglia, Leo. *Love*. New York: Fawcett Crest, 1972.

Jampolsky, Gerald. *Love Is Letting Go of Fear*. New York: Bantam, 1970.

Viscott, David. *The Language of Love*. New York: Pocket Books, 1976.

Meditations

Epstein, Gerald. *Healing Visualizations*. New York: Bantam, 1989.

Gawain, Shakti. *Creative Visualization*. San Rafael, CA: New World Library, 1978.

La Berge, Stephen. *Lucid Dreaming*. New York: Ballantine, 1985.

Men's Issues

Farrell, Warren. *Why Men Are the Way They Are*. New York: Berkely, 1986.

Friday, Nancy. *Men in Love, Men's Sexual Fantasies: The Triumph of Love Over Rage*. New York: Dell, 1980.

Goldberg, Herb. *The Hazards of Being Male: Surviving the Myth of Masculine Privilege*. New York: Signet, 1976.

Goldberg, Herb. *The Inner Male.* New York: Signet, 1987.

Kiley, Dan. *The Peter Pan Syndrome.* New York: Dodd, Mead and Co., 1983.

Lew. *Victims No Longer.* New York: HarperCollins, 1990. (For male victims of sexual abuse.)

Pruett, Kyle. *The Nurturing Father.* New York: Warner, 1987.

Relationships

Branden, Nathaniel. *If You Could Hear What I Cannot Say.* New York: Bantam, 1983.

Cowen, Connell, and Melvyn Kinder. *Smart Women, Foolish Choices.* New York: Clarkson N. Potter, 1985.

Forward, Susan, and Joan Torres. *Men Who Hate Women and the Women Who Love Them: When Loving Hurts and You Don't Know Why.* New York: Bantam, 1986.

Johnson, Robert. *He.* New York: Harper and Row, 1974.

Johnson, Robert. *She.* New York: Harper and Row, 1976.

Levin-Shneidman, Conalee, and Karen Levine. *Too Smart for Her Own Good? The Impact of Success on the Intimate Lives of Women.* New York: Doubleday, 1985.

Norwood, Robin. *Women Who Love Too Much: When You Keep Wishing and Hoping He'll Change.* New York: Jeremy P. Tarcher, 1985.

Rubin, Lillian. *Intimate Strangers.* New York: Harper and Row, 1983.

Silverstein, Shel. *The Missing Piece.* New York: Harper and Row, 1976.

Silverstein, Shel. *The Missing Piece Meets the Big O.* New York: Harper and Row, 1981.

Self-Growth

Beattie, Melody. *Codependent No More.* New York: Harper and Row, 1987.

Beattie, Melody. *Beyond Codependency.* New York: Harper and Row, 1989.

Lazaris. *The Sacred Journey: You and Your Higher Self.* Palm Beach, FL: NPN Publishing, Inc., 1987.

Lazaris. *Lazaris Interviews Book I.* Palm Beach, FL: NPN Publishing, Inc., 1988.

Lazaris. *Lazaris Interviews Book II.* Palm Beach, FL: NPN Publishing, Inc., 1988.

Spirituality

Lazaris. *The Sacred Journey: You and Your Higher Self.* Palm Beach, FL: NPN Publishing, Inc., 1987.

Roberts, Jane. *Seth Speaks.* New York: Bantam, 1972.

Starhawk. *The Spiral Dance: A Rebirth of the Ancient Religion of the Great Goddess.* New York: Harper and Row, 1979.

Walker, Barbara. *The Woman's Encyclopedia of Myths and Secrets.* New York: Harper and Row, 1983.

Success

Harvey, Joan. *If I'm So Successful Why Do I Feel Like a Fake? The Imposter Syndrome.* New York: Pocket Books, 1985.

Levin-Shneidman, Conalee, and Karen Levine. *Too Smart for Her Own Good? The Impact of Success on the Intimate Lives of Women.* New York: Doubleday, 1985.

Ross, Ruth. *Prospering Woman: A Complete Guide to Achieving the Full Abundant Life.* Mill Valley, CA: Whatever Publishing, 1982.

Women's Issues

Boston Women's Health Collective. *The New Our Bodies, Ourselves: A Book by and for Women.* New York: Simon and Schuster, 1984.

Eisler, Riane. *The Chalice and the Blade.* New York: Harper and Row, 1987.

Friedan, Betty. *The Feminine Mystique.* New York: Dell, 1983.

Nin, Anaïs. *The Diary of Anaïs Nin, Volume I*, ed. Gunther Stuhlmann. New York: Harvest/HBJ, 1966.

Nin, Anaïs. *The Diary of Anaïs Nin, Volume II*, ed. Gunther Stuhlmann. New York: Harvest/HBJ, 1969.

Nin, Anaïs. *The Diary of Anaïs Nin, Volume III*, ed. Gunther Stuhlmann. New York: Harvest/HBJ, 1969.

Walker, Barbara. *The Woman's Encyclopedia of Myths and Secrets*. New York: Harper and Row, 1983.

Walker, Barbara. *The Crone, Woman of Age, Wisdom and Power*. New York: Harper and Row, 1985.

INDEPENDENCE

Bloom, Lynn. *The New Assertive Woman*. New York: Dell, 1975.

Dowling, Colette. *The Cinderella Complex: Women's Secret Fear of Independence*. New York: Summit, 1981.

Fezler, William. *The Good Girl Syndrome*. New York: Macmillan, 1985.

Kiley, Dan. *The Wendy Dilemma: When Women Stop Mothering Their Men*. New York: Avon, 1984.

Kolbenschlag, Madonna. *Kiss Sleeping Beauty Good-bye*. New York: Bantam, 1979.

SEXUALITY

Barbach, Lonnie. *For Yourself: The Fulfillment of Female Sexuality*. New York: Doubleday, 1975.

Barbach, Lonnie. *Shared Intimacies*. New York: Bantam, 1980.

Hite, Shere. *The Hite Report: A Nationwide Study of Female Sexuality*. New York: Dell, 1976.

Vare, Ethlie. *Mothers of Invention*. New York: Morrow, 1988.

KIMBERLEY
H E A R T
NLIMITED

ORDER FORM
Books

When Fairy Tale
Romances Break
Real Hearts $12.95 ea. Quantity____ $_____

Signed Copy $17.95 ea. Quantity____ $_____

Audio Tapes
UnlimitedGrowth Series

When Fairy Tale Romances
Break Real Hearts
Meditation Tape $15 ea. Quantity____ $_____

A Touch of Heart Series
(includes booklet and meditation tape)

Introducing the
Old Man $15 ea. Quantity____ $_____

Introducing the
Anima $15 ea. Quantity____ $_____

Introducing the
Child-Self $15 ea. Quantity____ $_____

TO ORDER DIRECT BY PHONE: **(818) 781-4769**

Payment Options:
  Amount enclosed $_____
  Check or Money Order
  Visa/Mastercard #_____   Exp. date _____
    Exact name printed on card_____
    Signature as on card_____

Please send my order to: (please print)
Name_____Phone (____)_____
Address_____
City_____State_____Zip_____

Shipment will be made upon receipt of your payment.
Send payment along with this form to:

> Kimberley Heart Unlimited
> 6000 Woodman Avenue
> Suite A/Dept. S
> Van Nuys, CA 91401

Kimberley Heart also gives seminars, workshops, and
lectures throughout the country on Romantic Relationships, Corporate Management, and UnlimitedGrowth.
Call or write for Kimberley's current workshop and
seminar schedule.

Shipping and Handling:

Order Size	Charge
Under $15.00	$3.85
$15.01-$30.00	$4.50
$30.01-$50.00	$5.90
$50.01-$75.00	$6.90
Over $75.00	$7.50
For UPS 2nd Day Air: Add $6.00 to	above charges

BOOKS THAT TRANSFORM LIVES

FROM H J KRAMER INC

WAY OF THE PEACEFUL WARRIOR
by Dan Millman
A tale of transformation and adventure . . .
a worldwide best-seller.

SACRED JOURNEY OF THE PEACEFUL WARRIOR
by Dan Millman
"After you've read SACRED JOURNEY, you will know
what possibilities await you."—WHOLE LIFE TIMES

NO ORDINARY MOMENTS
by Dan Millman
Drawing on the premise that to change our world we first have
to change ourselves, Dan shares an approach to life that turns
obstacles into opportunities, and experiences into wisdom.

MESSENGERS OF LIGHT:
THE ANGELS' GUIDE TO SPIRITUAL GROWTH
by Terry Lynn Taylor
At last, a practical way to connect with the
angels and to bring heaven into your life!

GUARDIANS OF HOPE:
THE ANGELS' GUIDE TO PERSONAL GROWTH
by Terry Lynn Taylor
More than sixty practical angel practices that lead to
more joy, hope, fun, love, and adventure in everyday life.

TALKING WITH NATURE
by Michael J. Roads
"From Australia comes a major new writer . . . a magnificent book!"
—RICHARD BACH, Author, *Jonathan Livingston Seagull*

JOURNEY INTO NATURE
by Michael J. Roads
"If you only read one book this year, make that book
JOURNEY INTO NATURE."—FRIEND'S REVIEW

SIMPLE IS POWERFUL
by Michael J. Roads
Embarking on a search for meaning and freedom
in their lives, Michael and Treenie discover that
answers are often deceptively simple.

BOOKS THAT TRANSFORM LIVES

FROM H J KRAMER INC

THE EARTH LIFE SERIES
by Sanaya Roman
*A course in learning to live with joy,
sense energy, and grow spiritually.*

LIVING WITH JOY, BOOK I
*"I like this book because it describes the way I feel
about so many things."*—VIRGINIA SATIR

PERSONAL POWER THROUGH AWARENESS:
A GUIDEBOOK FOR SENSITIVE PEOPLE, BOOK II
"Every sentence contains a pearl. . . ."—LILIAS FOLAN

SPIRITUAL GROWTH:
BEING YOUR HIGHER SELF, BOOK III
*Orin teaches how to reach upward to align with the
higher energies of the universe, look inward to expand
awareness, and move outward in world service.*

OPENING TO CHANNEL:
HOW TO CONNECT WITH YOUR GUIDE
by Sanaya Roman and Duane Packer, Ph.D.
*This breakthrough book is the first
step-by-step guide to the art of channeling.*

An Orin/DaBen Book
CREATING MONEY
by Sanaya Roman and Duane Packer, Ph.D.
*This best-selling book teaches
advanced manifesting techniques.*

IN SEARCH OF BALANCE
by John Robbins and Ann Mortifee
*An inquiry into issues and concerns of the heart from
the best-selling author of DIET FOR A NEW AMERICA.*

THE COMPLETE HOME GUIDE TO AROMATHERAPY
by Erich Keller
*An easy-to-use guide to aromatherapy that opens
the door to the magical world of natural scents.*

YOU THE HEALER: THE WORLD-FAMOUS SILVA METHOD
ON HOW TO HEAL YOURSELF AND OTHERS
by José Silva and Robert B. Stone
*YOU THE HEALER is the complete course in
the Silva Method healing techniques presented
in a do-it-yourself forty-day format.*